BRING ON THE
CLOWNS

. . . it is an error of human judgement to regard humour as essentially trivial.   G. WILSON KNIGHT

The clown stands on his head and sees the world the right way up.   FR. BILL SARGENT, former chaplain of Holy Trinity, Dalston, London, the clowns' church

It is meat and drink to me to see a clown.   TOUCHSTONE in *As You Like It*

BRING ON THE
CLOWNS

BERYL HUGILL

CHARTWELL
BOOKS INC.

Published by Chartwell Books Inc
A Division of Book Sales Inc
110 Enterprise Avenue
Seacaucus, New Jersey 07094

© Beryl Hugill 1980

ISBN 0-89009-343-1
Library of Congress Catalog Card Number 80-80394

Typeset in Great Britain and printed in the United States of America

Contents

Acknowledgements

No book can be written without a certain amount of help and encouragement, and this volume is no exception. My first thanks are extended to all the clowns who have so generously and tolerantly given me their time, in particular David Barnes (Barney the Magic Clown) of London and Bert Sikorski (Trebla) of Baltimore. I am indebted also to friends who took an active interest in the book, among them R. F. D. Green of Washington, and to a colleague of my husband— Jack Lonsdale, Head of Intelligence, *The Times*. I am grateful, also, for the kind and efficient help given to me by the staffs of the British Library and the Westminster City Library in Marylebone; and Robert L. Parkinson, Chief Librarian and Historian, Circus World Museum, Barabou, Wisconsin.

Finally, on behalf of all clowns, I would like to pay tribute to Charlie Cairoli, the French-born clown, who died last month at the age of seventy after a lifetime in the circus. Between matinée and evening show of a pantomime at the New Theatre, Oxford, in which he was appearing, Charlie spent an hour talking to me of his art and convinced me of the sheer professionalism of the serious business of being a clown. To him, there was no such thing as a bad audience, only a bad clown.

BERYL HUGILL
March 1980

1 Introducing the Clown

Step out of the Paris Métro at Filles-du-Calvaire and you are in the Marais quarter, one of the toughest working-class districts of the city. Facing you is an enchanting sight which stands out against the dingy shopfronts and seedy dwellings. It is the fairy-tale building of the Cirque d'Hiver, its portals guarded by two glittering gilded statues of Roman horsemen. Since the circus was first opened by Napoleon III in 1852 it has been the home of great clowns. On a bitterly cold January night the Bouglione Circus is showing here.

Henri Dantes has coolly presented his performing lions, and the ringboys are busy dismantling the cage. Into the spotlight springs the droll, gangling figure of YoYo, the carpet clown, with a small box in his hands. He seats himself on one side of the ringfence and with a happy little shrug brings the audience straightaway into some kind of mischievous conspiracy. The clown slowly lifts up the lid of the box and the circus band strikes up the tinkling strains of a music-box tune. In strides the ringmaster. In mock anger he snatches away the box, ostentatiously snaps shut the lid, and hands it back. Once the ringmaster has left, YoYo goes to another part of the ring and repeats his performance, only to be frustrated yet again by the even angrier ringmaster. The clown's mouth turns down in the saddest of expressions. As soon as the ringmaster has made his exit once more, the clown perks up and plays his music-box for yet another section of the surrounding audience. On this occasion the ringmaster strides purposefully towards him, takes away the box and then stamps on it, breaks it apart and throws the resulting mess into a dustbin which has suddenly appeared in the ring. Off he stomps. The dejected clown ambles slowly towards the bin. He looks round surreptitiously before he snatches off the dustbin cover. Seemingly from out of the bin comes the gay melody of the music-box. Hardly able to believe it, the clown slams down the lid, then lifts it, and the tune is heard again. His face wreathed in smiles, he leaves the ring, the bin cradled lovingly under one arm and the lid raised in triumph by the other while the melody plays on.

Up to this point the watching members of the audience have been completely silent, spellbound. Now they laugh and cheer, utterly charmed into good humour and ready to watch any death defying act the circus has to bring. Meanwhile, the ringboys have quietly done their stuff; the arena is clear for the next artists.

The lights dim and we hear the bold sound of a trumpet. The spotlight picks out the musician who stands on a seat near the band. It is the awesome figure of the white clown. His face and neck are covered in white make-up with touches here and there of red and black. He wears a white conical hat, white shoes and stockings and a magnificent shimmering red-sequinned coat. He is joined by his two partners, who look rather less than magnificent. Their clothes are ill-fitting;

'Get away you clown; I want none of your buffoonery' (*BBC Hulton Picture Library*)

7

Les Brizios come unstuck in the traditional bill-pasting sketch
(*Douglas Dickins*)

they wear floppy shapeless hats, outsize shoes and gaudily striped stockings; one sports a red wig. Wide smiles are painted on their faces and they wear red false noses.

This is the French clown *équipe* Les Pauwels. Peppet, father of the clown family, has been performing at the Cirque d'Hiver since 1924. One son, Charlot, was born here and the other, Marquis, the white clown, came into the world while the family was travelling with a tenting circus in South America. Typical of many Continental clown troupes, Les Pauwels base their act on the fine nineteenth-century tradition of the Fratellini brothers. The white clown is always superior, never in trouble, untouched by water or custard pies. His first partner, the auguste, appears stupid and clumsy, but he has a fair share of cunning and comes out top in the end. His second partner is the contre-auguste, whose grotesque slow-wittedness is unredeemed; he is the butt of every joke.

The three clowns have made their way into the ring through the audience. The augustes make a play of losing their hats and tripping over their giant shoes.

8

Circus artists are often expected to do odd jobs as well as their act in the ring. Here, Australian clown Doug Buchal keeps his eye on fifteen-month-old Gene Harrison, a sixth-generation member of the Sole Brothers Circus family (*Sun Herald*)

The White Clown of Venice from *La Grande Eugène*, the show designed and directed by Franz Salieri and seen at the Roundhouse, London, in 1977 (*John Topham Picture Library*)

For the moment, they have abandoned their musical instruments. There is more fun to be had as the white clown commandeers the augustes and asks them to hold up a lighted candle in a candlestick. It is to be a pistol target. The first clown will have none of it and with great ooh-ing and aah-ing flees the scene to leave the task to his partner. Calmly the auguste takes hold of the candlestick. While the white clown turns his back to reload his gun, he slowly consumes the entire candle and candlestick, which is obviously edible. There is much smacking of lips and licking of fingers. He wipes his mouth with the sleeve of his coat and burps. The white clown is ready. He turns and aims his pistol at what he hopes is the target, but it has disappeared. He utters a stream of loud complaints as the auguste turns nonchalantly towards the artists' exit, revealing to the audience the fate of the candle: a small light gleams from between his coat-tails.

The clowns at the Cirque d'Hiver provide fun for others besides Parisians; like all good clowns, they have a universal appeal and can draw laughter from audiences all over the world. This is mainly because in clowning spoken language is more or less redundant. Whatever language we speak, the antics of the clown are readily understandable to us. Quite commonly, clowns speak several languages, but their performances consist almost entirely of visual humour.

This is not to say that there are no talking clowns. English clowns who went to France in the late nineteenth century actually made a joke of their difficulties with the French tongue. An early circus clown, Billy Saunders, murdered the phrase 'Voulez-vous jouer avec moi?' so hilariously that his pronunciation became the trademark of his successors, the *clowns parleurs*. 'Volé-vô joer avé moâ?' was always greeted with shrieks of laughter. A Victorian clown called William Wallett seems never to have stopped talking. His routine featured long quotations from Shakespeare, sometimes in recitations but also in witty exchanges with the ringmaster. The great Swiss clown Grock, although more famous for his musical eccentricities than for verbal jokes, used grotesque pronunciation to great effect, as when he absurdly lengthened the last syllable of 'Pourquoi . . .' Dicky Usher, one of the best known early circus clowns, was unique in that he used jokes written for him free of charge by pupils of Westminster School.

One characteristic of clowns is that they do not use a script. There are standard routines, some very ancient, which are passed on from clown to clown; dialogue for them is rarely, if ever, written down. When one reads the few routines which have been set down, it is impossible to appreciate their humour without the magic ability of the clown to give them life. The key element is improvisation, rather than the scenario on which it is based—a tradition that goes back to the commedia dell'arte of Renaissance Italy.

In the circus visual humour is most important. Some circuses can hold as many as 20,000 people, and many spectators will be too far away from the arena to hear what is said. So the clown employs a multitude of skills which he has learned at a very young age in order to speak to us without words. He may be able to juggle, ride, walk the tight-rope, train animals or do balancing and trapeze acts and acrobatics as well as any serious artist. He may interrupt and parody other acts, in which case he is called a reprise clown. The entrée clown (called the production clown in America) will perform with a troupe and use a variety of props which range from a simple bucket of water or leaky umbrella to a comedy car or a house on fire. Traditionally, the entrée is performed by the white clown and his auguste partners. The clown to whom falls the task of

opposite right: Scottish clown Don Sanders in his famous bagpipe sketch at the re-opening of the Cirque d'Hiver, Paris, in November 1969 (*Keystone Press Agency*)

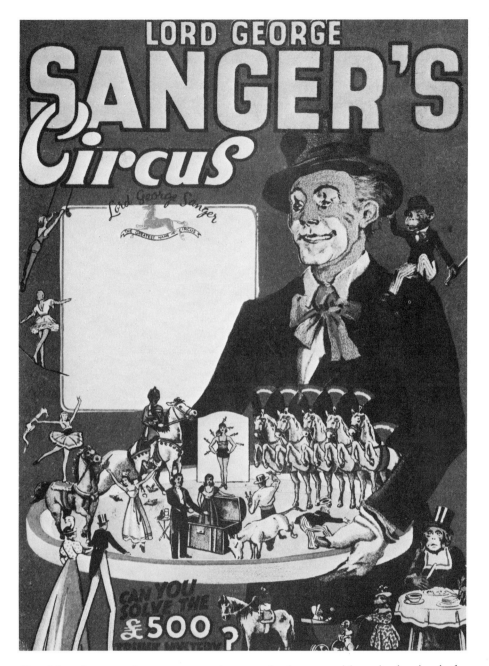

A bill poster for 'Lord' George Sanger's circus (*BBC Hulton Picture Library*)

disguising the prop changes or covering up mistakes or accidents in the ring is the carpet or run-in clown. He can be, and often is, much more than a glorified scene-shifter. What makes the clown special is an individual, highly eccentric personality whose main aim is to get the audience on his side in his struggles against tyrannical ringmasters, rebellious animals and the unpredictability of a whole variety of inanimate objects.

Not every clown, of course, comes from the circus. Two of the greatest clowns of the past made their names in the theatre. The Swiss clown Grock made a fortune by his success on the music hall stage. Joseph Grimaldi was exclusively a genius of the English pantomime. The circus as we know it was in its infancy when Grimaldi was delighting audiences at London's Drury Lane and Covent Garden Theatres in the late eighteenth and early nineteenth centuries. Grimaldi's unique invention was a satirical, urban clown whose

opposite left: Francesco Cairoli looks at a unique collection of eggs on which the faces of more than eighty clowns have been recorded. The exhibition was held in London in 1968 to mark the two-hundredth anniversary of the first circus. The egg collection is in private hands in Britain (*John Topham Picture Library*)

13

memory is kept alive in the term that circus people use for clowns, 'Joeys'. Joey's rumbustious clown character could not have been more different from that other great stage clown, Jean-Gaspard Deburau, the very model of the moon-faced, melancholy Pierrot.

The actual word 'clown' did not enter the language until the sixteenth century. It is of Low German origin and means a countryman or peasant. Its original meaning is allied in sense to the word for a Dutch or German farmer, 'boor', from which we get the adjective 'boorish'. So 'clown' meant someone who was doltish or ill-bred. In the Middle Ages comical entertainers, both at court and among the common people, were called by a variety of names denoting their various styles of clowning. There were jongleurs, minstrels, joculators, fools, jesters, mummers, mountebanks, zanies and the buffoonish players of the miracle and mystery plays. Before the Norman Conquest Anglo-Saxon England had been entertained by glee-men, poetical musicians who added humour to their songs of bravery and virtue. Often assisted by glee-maidens, they also used dancing as well as sleight-of-hand to amuse their audiences. The arrival of the Normans drove the glee-men underground, and when their artistic descendants emerged in the fourteenth century it was in a less respected form, akin to wandering minstrels and buffoons.

There has always been a large condescension in attitudes towards clowns. The court jester was a fool licensed to speak his mind only in the disguise of nonsense. The most wicked despot would accept criticism from his jester which in the mouths of his knights would result in summary execution. This tolerance stemmed from the belief that idiots were divine and that their presence formed a magic protection from evil. Consequently, royal households generally included an imbecile, for entertainment as well as protection.

The mentally defective entertainer was termed an 'innocent'. He was treated with great kindness—if one ignores the cruelty implicit in laughing at the handicapped. His clothes were the rich garments of the courtier, or the distinctive cap and bells, and he was showered with largesse. Not surprisingly, most of these supposed 'innocents' were of perfectly sound mind—'artificial' rather than 'natural' fools, in the parlance of the day. After all, court jesters enjoyed great power; they were often closer to the ear of the monarch than the most favoured baron. The astute 'artificial' fool pretended to imbecility in order to carve for himself a most attractive niche where the sole crime was to fail to amuse.

Clowns were very much a part of Elizabethan theatre. Those in the plays of Shakespeare, Robert Greene, Thomas Dekker and others were essentially country boobies. The clown played little part in the action of the drama; he was there by popular demand. Dressed in russet costume and speaking with a country burr, this simple yokel would be by turns gluttonous, thieving, naive and idiotic. He was obviously not fit company for a king; it was the court jester— in Elizabethan drama as in real life—who provided comic entertainment for royalty. In the hands of Shakespeare the court fool acquired another dimension and served to sharpen the themes of the plays. To Shakespeare, the fool was the voice of realism in a world where affectation, ambition, fashionable melancholy and madness reigned.

Make-up has always been part of clowning. Its long tradition goes back to the Dionysian mimes of ancient Greece, who daubed soot or grapejuice on their faces as they danced in celebration of the wine harvest. Mime actors in farces in ancient Greece and in the Roman Empire used grotesque masks to denote

various comic types. Modern clown faces most probably derived from a later source. The white face is said to have originated in early seventeenth-century Paris, where a baker named Gros-Guillaume (Fat William) was applauded for his low comic acting in farces. He performed at fairs and, later, with renowned theatre companies at the Hôtel de Bourgogne, his face still covered in flour after a strenuous day's work. Audiences were amused by his habit of blowing the flour off his face and nicknamed him *le fariné*. The practice of wearing a white face was popularized by later clowns at French fairs and was adopted by Deburau at the Funambules Theatre in Paris. Nineteenth-century white clowns added touches of red and black to caricature the shape of their own faces. The modern clown adds all kinds of weird squiggles, commas, tears and triangles to the basic white make-up. The faces of street clowns and American circus clowns are particularly inventive.

The auguste is never complete without his bulbous rubber nose. This practice stemmed from the nineteenth-century augustes who would paint their noses red if they wished to portray a drunk. The monstrously grotesque make-up of some augustes was initiated by Albert, the youngest of the Fratellini brothers. Whereas early augustes had worn very little make-up, Albert painted large white areas around his mouth and eyes, coloured his lips, exaggerated his eyebrows with black and added touches of colour to his cheeks. This tradition is carried on by many modern clowns, such as Lou Jacobs, who also wears the red wig of the early augustes. There are some clowns today who are using less and less make-up. Some say this is to make the clown appear less frightening. In Eastern Europe

A Roman masked actor as (*left*) Bucco, the bragging comic figure of ancient Roman comedy and (*right*) Pappus, the old man character of the Atellan farces (*BBC Hulton Picture Library*)

15

and Russia it is part of an attempt to present the clown's comedy as realistic and dignified rather than surrealistic and ridiculous.

The Russian clown, Oleg Popov, wears hardly any make-up at all, save for a touch under the nose to emphasize its *retroussé* shape. Charlie Cairoli painted on spiky black eyebrows and a small moustache in addition to a red, false nose; the rest of his face was flesh coloured. The effect is eccentric and amusing rather than fearfully grotesque. There is a recognizable human identity, too, in the basic face of the tramp or hobo clown. The doleful unshaven face and reddened nose of the tramp clown is an American tradition and was first popularized in the circus by the late Emmett Kelly.

Each clown's face is unique—a variation on the basic type of clown he portrays. In order to record their faces in the days before photography clowns used to paint them on eggshells. It was an informal way of claiming copyright of a clown disguise.

Today, as in the past, the backgrounds of the people who become clowns cut right across the social spectrum. Ringling Brothers and Barnum & Bailey Circus includes a graduate lawyer, the son of a judge, among its clowns, as well as a factory worker and a one-time speech therapist. Among students at this circus's Clown College are the sons and daughters of mayors, doctors, teachers, television producers and mechanics. The grandfather of Charlie Cairoli was a prime minister of Italy. Many of the performers in the commedia dell'arte were landowners and possessed a high level of intellectual ability. But many people feel that the best clowns are those born in a circus wagon, who at a young age begin the long and arduous apprenticeship in the clownish skills. To be born in the show run by a celebrated circus clan has always had much kudos; to be able to say you were a Fossett, a Chipperfield, a Rosaire or a Hanneford, to name just a few families, was and is something of which to be proud.

Modern times have seen a growing number of street clowns, many of them amateurs coming from all walks of life. There is an increasing use of the clown's burlesque and techniques in street and community theatre. Understandably, perhaps, there is much suspicion of this comparatively recent phenomenon among established clowns. This suspicion seems to be rooted in the feeling that street clowns do not take the business of being funny seriously enough. In many cases, this new breed of clown has not endured the years and years of training that the circus performer undergoes. It is not enough to borrow the clown's motley and to use his skills without the naturally comic personality which underlies all he does.

However, there is no doubt that young street clowns are very inventive. Not only do they brighten the landscape of our cities with their own brand of lunacy; they also—unlike the Western circus clown—readily tackle controversial and political subjects. Like the medieval entertainers, modern street clowns can be found wherever there is an audience to watch them: in market squares, at local galas and carnivals, in schools, at community centres, music festivals, rock concerts, horse shows and in parades.

Never, it seems, was there more interest in clowning than there is today. Many mime schools have sprung up in Europe and America, and the traditional clown training centres attract plenty of candidates. Interest in the Clown College, founded by Ringling Brothers and Barnum & Bailey Circus in 1968, has been growing fast, and the number of applicants runs at between 5,000 and 6,000 a year, coming from almost all parts of the world.

Although this photograph is signed 'O'Gust', a joking reference to the knockabout auguste clown, this French performer is closer to the tradition of the late nineteenth-century white clown (*Mander & Mitchenson Theatre Collection*)

Interestingly, more than half of these would-be clowns are women—a sharp break with tradition. Of course today, as in the past, there are many brilliant comic actresses; comediennes such as Beryl Reid and Mary Tyler Moore are as funny as any clown. But their humour is personal, related to the roles women are still expected to play in a man's world. Clowns, by contrast, tend to have a neuter quality, created in part by their often bizarre make-up and costume, and until recently women have not felt at ease or been convincing in such an asexual role. More naturally, some female clowns have taken the place of the male clown who would appear as a grotesque caricature of a woman in an entrée or run-in. For example, Peggy Williams, the first of the Ringling women clown graduates, appears in the satin and feathers of a burlesque Wild West saloon hostess. But now some women are succeeding as clowns of the traditionally neutral type. One of these is the Australian Nola Rae, whose work is presented by the London Mime Theatre. Her solo two-hour show played to packed houses throughout Britain in 1979. (In this book, incidentally, the pronoun 'he' is used in referring to a clown purely for convenience.)

It is much easier to specify what a clown does than to explain exactly what he is. Clowns must have been most irritated by that eternal reporter's question: 'Why did you become a clown?' Grock answers the question rather ungraciously in his autobiography by saying, 'Because I wanted to'. A rather more good-natured answer comes from a young English clown called Teddy Green, who joined the circus at the age of sixteen after an upbringing in Dover. 'I could have been a foreman road-sweeper for Dover Corporation', he observes, 'but clowning messed up all my career'. For many old-school clowns there was never very much choice. Those born into circus families were often dressed up and pushed on to the sawdust when they were tiny children. Other clowns may be former trapeze or high wire artists who have had an accident in the ring or are not fit enough to perform the strenuous acts they once did.

There is a school of thought that says the clown's mask hides deep unhappiness. The idea of the broken-hearted clown is a hard one to disregard, even though most clowns will emphatically tell you it is a myth. Many clowns have in common a hard or unsettled upbringing. Charlie Chaplin's childhood was spent in appalling poverty in London's East End; Grimaldi's young life was plagued by the excesses of a neurotically strict father. Travelling clowns were at the mercy of the elements, and the countries they performed in were often battered by wars and revolutions. In spite of modern Western affluence, many clowns still bear the scars of early deprivation. One English clown, aged a mere thirty-five, remembers a childhood in which he often went hungry and wandered about with holes in his shoes; he recalls a woman who dubbed him 'Oliver Twist'.

Clowns are obliged to make us laugh even when they are hit by the personal tragedies which may affect any human being. The later years of Grimaldi's life were greatly saddened by the untimely death of his only son through drink and later of his wife through illness; yet he never lost his faith in life and laughter. There are even tales of clowns who joked on their death-beds.

It is interesting that the Ringling Clown College is aware that a good clown has what is termed a 'sensitive background'. Some of the questions asked on the college's application form seem to suggest that the college believes clownish creativity has much to do with emotional sensibilities. The applicant is asked the last time he cried and why and to name the emotion he felt at the time. He is asked to describe his greatest personal crisis and how he dealt with it, to say whether he likes poetry and to indicate what sort of books he reads. And as if that is not enough, he is asked to say who in the world he would most like to be, given the opportunity—a question that recalls Woody Allen's remark that his one regret in life is that he was not born somebody else.

But the clown's private regrets are not visited upon us. The clown knows that he is not here to cheer himself up but to bring joy to his audience. He is only too well aware that there is a limit to the amount of gloom we can feel. For most of us, moods of sadness and despair have ultimately to lift, however dire the cause. The business of the clown is to help alleviate the iniquities of our society and the vulnerability of our human condition through laughter. This is not to say that the clown trivializes; some of the most trenchant points about life have been made by clowns and jesters. He is, rather, telling us universal truths about our own humanity which we can all recognize, with which we can reconcile ourselves and which bring us together.

The clown knows what it is to be the underdog, to be out of a job, to be done down by authority; but more than that, he knows he is not alone. In his magical and eccentric way, he triumphs through this self-knowledge. He transcends the buffeting, always gets up to live another day and shares his joy with us. However wealthy a nation, however democratic its government, the clown, fearless and free, will always be needed. For the clown is in essence a creature of love. Nobody, as Max Beerbohm said, ever died of laughter.

2 Laughter from the Distant Past

One of the fascinations of ancient people is that the things that made them laugh were not so very different from the ones that make us laugh today. Leaving aside humorous references to aspects of one society that would be meaningless in another time and place, there is a universality about clowning through the ages resulting from clowns' comparative freedom to mock all folly.

Different as their institutions and mores may have been from ours, the inhabitants of ancient Greece, Rome and Asia Minor loved to see them mocked—just as we mock our own. Political figures and monarchs were satirized mercilessly; and the more authoritarian and pompous they were, the better. The language of tragic drama was grist for the parodist's mill. Even religion was not exempt from mockery. And, as always, the foibles of common folk provided plenty of good material for the satirist and plenty of merriment for his appreciative audience.

Although there was patronage of clowns by king and state, the growth of clowning had its roots essentially in the life of ordinary people, arising out of rustic festivals and the celebration of the wine harvest. Clowns were, as they still are to some extent, the voice of the people, an expression of human feeling.

It was in ancient Egypt, so far as we know, that the clown first appeared, some five thousand years ago. This early type of clown was the danga, a member of a tribe of pygmies who was kept in the households of noble and royal families. The danga would amuse his masters by dancing and imitating their gods, one of which was Bes, god of the dance and battles. Wearing a leopard skin, the danga would, it was said, 'divert the court and rejoice the heart of the king'. The Egyptians were very much amused by dwarfism and deformity. If this seems a degraded kind of humour to us, we can remind ourselves of the midget waddling across the modern circus ring. To the Egyptians the danga was as much a magical charm against ill fortune as a source of amusement. He was regarded with a kind of primitive wonder.

As we have seen, much of a clown's performance depends on improvisation. Improvisation was a strong element in the art of the ancient Greek clown. He was one of the stock figures in popular farces based on mythological themes developed in the cities of Megara and Sparta in southern Greece. The farcical play was termed a *phlyake*. The clown who appeared in it would wear tights, a short tunic or *chiton* with half sleeves and would be grotesquely padded back and front; an exaggerated artificial phallus would be strapped round his loins. His shaven head glistened and his face was daubed with paint or soot. In common with the tragic actors, the clowns wore masks with yawning open mouths which amplified their voices.

The humour of Greek clowns was of a rough and ready kind, totally improvised at first. The clown might play a thievish comic slave character or a

A satyr with wine skin, c. 500 BC. Satyrs were usually depicted wearing the ears and tails of goats or horses, and were much given to Bacchic revelry, a primitive ritual celebration of the wine harvest (*BBC Hulton Picture Library*)

foolish doctor. Herakles, or Hercules, was a most popular figure, and buffoonish portrayals of his legendary exploits were a favourite entertainment. Other stock types included an old man with a pointed beard and an ancient, hag-like woman. Back-chat and ribald exchanges between clowns and the audience formed a large part of the fun, climaxed when the clowns threw basketfuls of nuts at the onlookers.

Some clowns wore animal heads—the most popular of which was the cock's head. The theatrical historian, Allardyce Nicoll (in *Masks, Mimes and Miracles*), believes that the cockscomb of the medieval fool may have descended from this disguise. The cock was considered a stupid, vain and libidinous creature and the character wearing this headdress would be interpreted as having the same traits.

Greek vases dating from around 800 BC are painted with representations of these grotesque fools, wearing crowns of ivy and blossoms and well padded, dancing with abandon in the worship of Dionysus, the god of wine. One of them could very well have been the Alexandrian clown, Matreas, popular with both Greeks and Romans. He is said to have burlesqued the logical problems set by Aristotle. 'Why does the sun descend and not set off swimming again?' he would ask, or, 'Why do sponges drink together and not get drunk?'

As with any entertainment that wins great popular favour, the farces and their buffoons had their critics. One of them was Aristophanes, who wrote the following address at the start of his comedy, *The Wasps*:

You're not going to get any crude Megarian stuff here. And I'm afraid we can't run to a couple of slaves with baskets full of nuts to throw at the spectators. You won't see Herakles being cheated of his dinner. We're not going to sling any mud at Euripides; and we don't intend to make mincemeat of Cleon.

Euripides was, of course, the great tragedian, and Cleon an Athenian politician and general who defeated the Spartans in 425 BC.

One of the things that makes us laugh at modern clowns is incongruity: Charlie Chaplin wears a tiny hat and enormous shoes; the clumsy auguste is always in trouble, never in harmony with the untouchable white clown. In these low comedies so beloved by the Greeks, brawny, strong, heroic Herakles would seem to be the equal of the bizarrely garbed rustic fool, rather than the superior he was supposed to be.

Like the Egyptians, noble and wealthy Greeks employed clowns for domestic entertainment. In return for their wit, repartee and mimicry these *parasites*, as the Greeks called them, would enjoy much favour and patronage. They were in great demand at banquets, which they visited in a peripatetic fashion, using their powers to amuse as a kind of currency. There were some with established positions in particular households, but many more simply hung round the baths and market places, touting for invitations.

Parasites were accorded nicknames just like medieval and modern clowns. Among them were Lark, Mackerel, Pod and Ham-cleaver. Some of their jests were written down. One of the first of these accounts of a clown's act comes from the writings of Xenophon (c. 430-355 BC), the Greek general and writer, and concerns a buffoon named Philip. Philip presented himself unasked at a feast held by Callias, where Socrates was leading serious moral debates, and gave this excuse for his temerity: 'Gentlemen, you all know me and my professional

privilege. But I have come uninvited chiefly because I have an aversion from ceremony, and a disinclination to put you to the trouble of a formal invitation'.

Philip was asked to amuse the banqueters but he was unable to raise even a giggle. It was only when he feigned a broken heart and was about to die with shame at his lack of success or their dullness, that his audience broke into laughter. At the banquet was a Syracusan dancing girl, one of whose tricks was to leap through a hoop in which knives were planted, pointing inwards. Philip used this as an opportunity to make a dig at an Athenian alderman who belonged to the peace party of his day: 'Ah, what pleasure should I enjoy to see Pisander, that grave counsellor, taking lessons from this girl; he that is ready to swoon away at the sight of a lance, and says it is a barbarous custom to go to war and kill men!'

Philip's blunt outspokenness was tolerated. His wit was not always spontaneous, however, and like other *parasites* he studied the jest books. A story is told of how Philip paid a large sum of money to 'The Sixty', an Athenian club of wits who had set down their own jests in a book. These jokes were often recognized by the company he entertained and groans met the telling of an 'old sixty', just as today we speak of a hoary old chestnut.

Another celebrated Greek *parasite* was Herodotus (not to be confused with the historian), who delighted audiences with his savage impressions of kings, fencers, singers and orators. The Syrian king Antiochus II counted Herodotus among his friends, and at a feast held in AD 168 the entertainer appeared in costume among the jesters and performed with them. Just as the British ruling class gathered to hear themselves wittily insulted by the satirists in the old

A Bacchanalian procession. Bacchus, the god of wine and fertility, was better known as Dionysus to the Hellenic world. The club and lion skin worn by the actor on the left always identified Herakles, a favourite butt for Greek humour. From a Greek marble relief in the Louvre (*BBC Hulton Picture Library*)

21

A Greek comedy actor from the first or second century AD. Masks were worn to convey emotion to an audience sitting some distance from the stage in a vast auditorium, much as a clown today uses grotesque make-up and wigs to catch attention in a big circus tent (*Mansell Collection*)

Establishment Club of London in the 1960s, so learned and aristocratic Greeks accepted a similar freedom of plain speaking from their fools. The following excerpt from Aristophanes' play *The Clouds* gives some idea of this licence:

Unjust cause: Now then tell me: from what class do the lawyers come?
Just cause: From the scoundrels.
Unjust: Very good! And the public speakers?
Just: Oh, from the scoundrels, also.
Unjust: And now look; which class is most common among our audience?
Just: I am looking.
Unjust: But what do you see?
Just: By all the gods, I see more scoundrels than anything else. That fellow, I particularly know; and him over there; and that scoundrel with the long hair.

The Greek clown—this irreverent mirth-maker who poked fun at heroes, at political and intellectual life and at the common people—soon acquired a counterpart in ancient Rome. Roman love of amusement is well known, and the clown was a popular source of entertainment there right up to the end of the Empire. Like well-born Egyptians, Romans kept midgets and freaks for amusement. Bronze models of dwarfs were carried around as good luck charms. The beginnings of the Roman clown proper emerged in crude stage performances in which a rustic booby would improvise farcical scenes, helped by the skilful antics of jugglers and acrobats.

These farces made their first appearance in the southern Italian town of Atella, which gave its name to a kind of mime play which was written for the players, the *fabula Atellana*. An essential feature of these farces was a high-spirited portrayal of traditional characters in ridiculous situations. The stock characters were called by the names of Bucco, Maccus, Pappus, Dossenus and Mandacus. Keeping in character, the actors would improvise humour on a given theme as the inspiration took them.

Maccus, along with Bucco, was a fool; he was a stupid, clumsy, blundering rustic; he was greedy, with peasant tastes in food. Mere fragments of the written mimes remain, but Maccus appears in a later play of Plautus. Before setting off on a long journey, the clumsy oaf bids farewell to his father's door: 'Lintel, whereon I have often banged my miserable head, Threshold, where I have stubbed all my toes!'

The character wore a square hood which could be drawn back or used for disguise as the plot demanded; his costume consisted of a patchwork jacket called a *centunculus*, tights and the phallus as worn in the Greek performances.

Bucco was the character renowned for his clownish wit. His puns, riddles and topical allusions were loved by Roman audiences. Over-literal interpretations on a serious character's remarks were particularly popular; when Bucco is asked to handle a job cleanly, he replies: 'I have already washed my hands.'

Pappus was a senile old man, with a wandering mind, often tricked by his younger companions. He was often lecherous, for along with adultery, Romans found the passions of old men very funny.

Dosennus was the cunning, wise fool character in the *fabula Atellana*. Along with Mandacus, he was the forerunner of Punch. A rather frightening humpbacked figure, he had a row of large teeth in a wide grinning mouth, a long hooked nose and an exaggerated jaw. Like the Greeks, Roman clowns often

portrayed animal types. The *cicirrus* was a cock. One story tells how the poet Horace, when a guest at a friend's villa, was entertained by two men, one called Sarmentus and the other Messius Cicirrus, who performed an animal mime.

From this story it is clear that Roman clowns entertained in private houses as well as on the improvised stages which were put up round the countryside for performance of the *fabulae Atellanae*. The players travelled from place to place like gipsies, setting up a wooden platform with a backstage curtain called the *siparium*.

The mimes are thought to have been performed in the middle of, or after, the main play, and the curtain would be used to hide the scenery while they took place. In fact, the clowns were probably used exactly as clowns are used in the circus today—that is, to take attention away from the changing of props and scenery. They may also have provided light relief after a particularly dramatic or tragic performance. In the beginning the buffoons performed on a platform in the orchestra, but as they became more and more popular they took over the main stage.

The performances came to be associated with civic festivals, one of which was held at Floralia from AD 283 onwards. It was here that the clown Latinus made his name. He was notorious for his indecent gestures and dress, and the games became a celebration of obscenity which included the denuding of women.

Latinus was what the Romans called a *sannio*, one of the most popular kinds of mimic. He was famous for his hilarious grimaces, so in all probability he did not wear a mask. The *sannio* would act with his body as well as with his face and his words. As with any gifted clown, he had only to move an arm or leg in a certain manner to have the audience smiling. Cicero once observed, 'It must be noted that not all ridiculous things are witty. What can be more ridiculous than the *sannio*? He arouses laughter by his face, his aspect, his manners, his voice, his very body itself'. Cleon, who lived about the same time as Latinus, was also a maskless clown and was described by a contemporary writer as 'the best maskless actor among the Italian mimes'.

Dramatic masks used in the Roman theatre (*BBC Hulton Picture Library*)

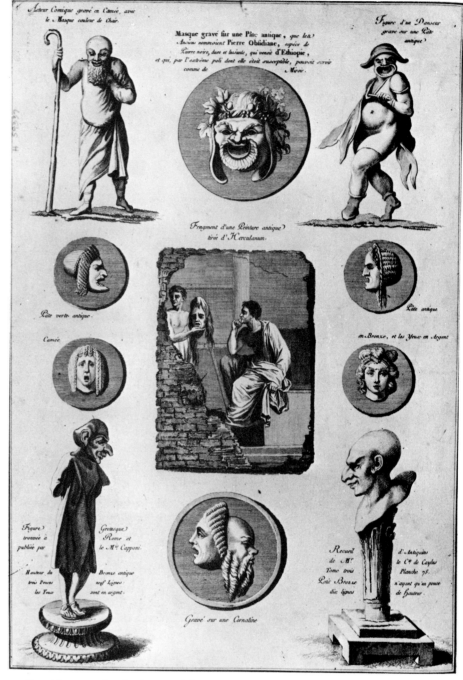

Stupidus was the Latin word for a mimic fool—a clown who would ape what the more serious actor had said. He would be bald-headed or wear a long pointed hat and a multi-coloured outfit of which the later Harlequin costume must be a direct descendant. The *stupidus* would rain blows on his fellow clowns in a burlesque fight in true slapstick fashion. He was also famed for his skill in riddles and innuendo. Nothing was sacred, and real-life scandals often provided the material. When the adulterous behaviour of the wife of the Emperor Aurelius became common knowledge, a *stupidus* on the stage asked a slave to tell him the name of an adulterer. The slave repeated three times a made-up name, 'Tullus'. When the *stupidus* asked him again, he replied, 'I have just told you thrice, Tullus'. (*Iam tibi dixi ter, Tullus.*) This was a pun on the name of the culprit,

Greek actors on stage (*Mansell Collection*)

Tertullus. This kind of allusion to the foibles of politicians and monarchs generally went unpunished.

A lower type of Roman clown was called the *scurra*, from which we get our word 'scurrilous'. The *scurra* indulged in jesting, and his physical oddities were more pronounced than in the better-class actors.

Emperors would bring clowns back as trophies from foreign lands, and some were, indeed, ex-slaves. One such clown was Publilius Syrus (from Syria), a writer as well as a gifted comic actor. He was awarded a prize by the Emperor Claudius for his clever wit. His good jokes and his graceful body won him not only his freedom but education and patronage as well. He became famous as a writer and actor of mimes throughout provincial Italy and in 46 BC went to the

25

Roman comedy was much broader and more ribald than the Greek New Comedy from which it stemmed. This scene comes from the fourth century BC (*Mansell Collection*)

public games, called *Ludi Caesaris*, to challenge his rivals and win Caesar's high esteem. Like the wise fools of Shakespeare's plays, Publilius Syrus brought a degree of sagacity to his foolery: 'Life is long for the wretched, short for the lucky', is one example of his aphorisms.

Despite their tendency to criticize the state, clowns were often much beloved and encouraged by Roman emperors. One such monarch was Commodus (reigned AD 180-192), who—although a mad tyrant—was a great enthusiast for all things theatrical. He himself was said to be something of an exhibitionist. According to contemporaries, he danced, sang, whistled and showed himself a perfect *scurra*; he was also a gladiator. Much of his property was bestowed on jesters and dancers. Heliogabalus, emperor for just four years before he was assassinated in AD 222, was very generous towards clowns, gave them money freely and pledged his royal credit for them. He was a very merry monarch and his roar of laughter was said to be so loud that it could drown all other sounds in the theatre.

A later emperor encouraged clowns to ridicule and make fun of the Christian religion. This was Julian, who, although educated as a Christian, tried to make the Roman Empire revert to paganism. One of his more eccentric enterprises was to organize mimic actors and clowns to perform revels for his soldiers over the entire plain of Ctesiphon, where he had been defeated by the Persians.

26

A Roman theatrical scene from a
fresco in Pompeii, and (*below*) this
second-century mosaic shows
strolling players, a customary
entertainment offered in wealthy
Roman households (*Mansell
Collection*)

27

Just as Rome adapted the Greek tradition of stage clowns, it also had its *parasites*. Gabba, the buffoon of the Emperor Augustus, was a permanent member of the household. Others enjoyed rather less exalted positions and used their wit in a mendicant fashion. In the Plautus play *Stichus*, or *The Parasite Rebuffed*, a *parasite* named Gelasimus, short of invitations, puts himself up for bidding: 'I've funny *bon mots* to sell. Come bid your price. Who bids a dinner? Ho! there, did you nod to me? No one will offer you better. I won't allow that any *parasite* has better quibbles, cajoleries and parasitical little perjuries.'

Clowns were not always beloved of Roman monarchs. The austere emperor Tiberius cracked down on the farces, after he had been referred to in one as 'an old he-goat'; their political satire had become a bit too incisive for his taste. In AD 22 Tiberius brought an order before the Senate suppressing the plays. However, the same style of entertainment continued at a later date; it was impossible to banish the clown, the champion of the common people against oppression. The *fabula Atellana*, once a provincial entertainment, became popular in Rome, where it flourished until the first century AD.

Although most clowns enjoyed immunity from punishment for mocking their so-called betters, a few of them were put to death. The unfortunate Agrippus, brought from Syria by the Emperor Verus and renamed Apolaustus ('The Enjoyable'), was later put to death by the Emperor Commodus, a sovereign who —though fond of high-jinks—did not have the same taste for satire as did his predecessor.

A nineteenth-century representation of a Roman comedy (*Mansell Collection*)

At least one clown became a victim of the persecution of Christians. This was Philemon, later made a saint. Philemon was a very popular figure in his home town of Antinoe in Egypt. During the reign of the Emperor Diocletian (AD 284-305) Christians were harassed, imprisoned and sometimes killed. It happened that in Antinoe there was a Christian deacon who was not the stuff of which martyrs are made. When asked to make the customary offering at the pagan altar, he asked Philemon to wear the priestly robes and to take his place, hoping to save himself. Philemon thought this a great joke, but when he arrived at the high court of Arianus, the prefect of the city, he suddenly announced that he was a Christian and refused to make the pagan sacrifice. At the same time, he pushed back his hood to reveal his true identity, at which the watching crowd roared with laughter. Arianus was prepared to let matters rest and dismiss the affair as a jest, albeit a risky one. But he soon saw that the clown was not joking

Itinerant Roman farce actors in a bas-relief from the Farnese Palace (*Mansell Collection*)

29

and that, if what he said was true, he would have to condemn this popular man to death. Arianus appealed to the crowd: 'What are we to do with this man? Shall we condemn him to instant death or is he to suffer lingering torment on the cross?' The people burst into tears. The prefect turned to Philemon and told him that he must have a heart of stone, if he were not moved by the people's display of love. Arianus begged the clown again and again to make his offering to the pagan gods. Philemon was adamant and condemned himself to death by his final words to the people he had once moved to laughter by his buffoonery: 'Good people of Antinoe, be not distressed at the blows I have received. I doubt not ye remember the time when I was a mime—how to my shame in the theatre blows were rained on me by my fellow actors. You laughed at those comic blows then, but the angels wept. Now, therefore, it is just that your tears should not weigh against the joy which the angels feel at my salvation.' Philemon's death by crucifixion was mourned as if he had been a great emperor.

In eastern lands the performing arts were not quite so separated as in the West. Dancing, music, acting, clowning, juggling and acrobatics were combined in ceremonies to celebrate the gods of fertility. In India this was the Hindu god Shiva, who represented the forces of both destruction and regeneration. The rites in honour of Shiva included processions of players dressed in parti-coloured costumes, beating on drums. The clown of the piece was always a Brahmin (a Hindu teacher) or a pupil of one. Among the minor characters was the *vita*. He wandered from palace to palace entertaining the nobility of India in much the same way as did the Greek *parasite*. He was usually a good musician who would compose and recite poetry, and his witty sayings were an essential part of his performance. A *vita* sometimes figured on the works of ancient Indian playwrights. More often, they included a character called the *vidusaka*. The *vidusaka* wore a mask over his face and a pair of comical wooden ears. He would pretend to be very greedy and simple. He tumbled about and shouted abuse at some of the other players. Indeed, the very word *vidusaka* means 'he who shouts abuse'.

It is believed there were jesters in China as early as the Chou dynasty (1027-221 BC), the classical period of Chinese history when the country's great schools of philosophy were founded. An early anecdote describes the acting ability of the chief jester of a Chinese court, who impersonated the mannerisms of a recently dead prime minister so well that the emperor was sure the minister had been restored to life.

Another story of a Chinese jester concerns the Great Wall. The clown in question was a man named Yu Sze, who lived some two thousand years ago and was jester to the Emperor Shih Huang-ti. It was this emperor who was respon-sible for building the 1,500-mile-long Great Wall to defend China's northern frontier. When it was completed, the emperor decided that it should be painted. This colossal task would have cost many lives, and taxes would have to be increased in order to meet the cost. No ordinary subject would have dared to criticize the emperor's decision; the task was left to Yu Sze, the only person who did not fear the royal wrath. The clown made such fun of the idea of painting the wall that the emperor finally gave up the project.

As well as at court, clowns amused people in the market-places and villages. They would mimic the manners of simple rustics and the antics of the towns-people. In the Chinese theatre serious plays continued for hours at a time. The patient audience was diverted in the middle of these long dramas by a pair of clowns who had nothing whatever to do with the plot. They would burst on to the stage and then disappear as swiftly as they had arrived, while the play continued as if nothing had happened. Rather like the modern white clown and his partner, these two Chinese clowns were counterparts. The *t'seng* was witty and commanding, while the *t'cheou* was rough and clumsy.

Other parts of the Far East also had their clowns. These countries were generally under despotic, aristocratic rule, and the clowns were the only spokesmen for the common man. They appeared as characters in plays, in which the heroes are gods, demi-gods, kings, princes and princesses and the other main characters priests and foreign adversaries. Comic relief was provided by the grotesque slapstick clowns, who served as confidants of their masters, aware of all their weaknesses and passions. As a counterpart to the lofty mythological themes of the dramas, the clowns commented irreverently on political or social issues of the time, improvising on the basic situation.

In Malaya, clowns similar to the ones who performed thousands of years ago still exist. They are called *p'rang* and are identified by huge masks and turbans half as big again as themselves.

Turkey celebrates the memory of a particularly endearing clown who, although an actual person, has become a folk hero and the subject of many stories—some of them rather tall, some joyously coarse. Going by the name of Nasr ed-Dîn, this clown lived 550 years ago as an imam, a kind of religious leader, in the town of Aqshehir in Asia Minor. He was celebrated for his curious blend of cunning, naivety, buffoonery and shrewdness; his main occupation in life was to score off other people and to play practical jokes. A fascinating account of this mischievous cleric appears in Sir Harry Luke's book *An Eastern Chequerboard*.

Nasr ed-Dîn was a court jester to Timur, or Tamburlaine, the Mongol conqueror. This terrifying man, who had conquered both the Tartars and the Turks while trying to unite the empire of Genghis Khan, had the misfortune to be lame and extremely ugly; he had also lost an eye during his exploits. The story goes that one day, as he was sitting with his jester and other courtiers, he chanced to scratch his head, noticed that his hair was rather long and called for the services of a barber. The barber duly shaved him and handed him a mirror to admire the finished result. Timur studied his face for a while and—dismayed by his ugliness—began to weep. Immediately, the courtiers began to weep with him in sympathy, but later they managed to talk him round and cheer him up by means of a few jokes. Meanwhile, Nasr ed-Dîn continued to weep even louder than before. Timur was astonished. 'I wept with reason at beholding my ugliness', he said. 'I the lord of so many lands, the master of countless slaves. But I do not understand why you should thus despair.'

Replied the jester: 'If you, my lord, wept for two hours after seeing yourself in the mirror for but an instant, is it not natural that I, who see you all day long, should weep longer than you?'

Timur's laughter at this witty riposte was almost uncontrollable.

In order to consolidate his popularity with Timur, the jester went to a nearby village, celebrated for the high quality of its geese, and cooked a goose for his master. On the way back, Nasr ed-Dîn felt hungry and ate one of the bird's legs. Timur was indignant when he was presented with the remains of the goose and wanted to know the whereabouts of the missing leg. The jester replied that in his country geese had only one leg and at the same time pointed to a flock of geese at a nearby pond, who, as it happened, were all standing on one leg. Timur ordered a drum to be beaten and the startled birds put down their other legs. The jester responded to this challenge by saying, 'I daresay that, if the drum were only beaten loudly enough, you could be made to stand on all fours!'

Nasr ed-Dîn wore a distinctive melon-shaped cap, stuffed with cotton, which is reproduced above his grave in Aqshehir. The site is a marble mausoleum in a graveyard. At the jester's request a small hole has been left in the masonry of the tomb, so that he can continue to look out upon the world. Above the grave hangs the ball he used to play with and the lock of his house, which he would not entrust to his wife, who now lies beside him.

As an imam, Nasr ed-Dîn was obliged to preach in the mosque, a task he heartily disliked. A story of the way he evaded this dreaded duty stands up very well to modern tastes in humour. One day he appeared in the pulpit and said to his eager congregation, 'O Moslems, do you know what I am going to say to you today?' 'No', they replied. 'No more do I', said the jester and left the mosque rapidly. The following week he asked the same question, but on this occasion the congregation replied 'Yes'. 'If you know then I needn't tell you', said the reluctant preacher and made good his escape once more. The next week the congregation thought they would outwit him, and in answer to his usual question they said, 'Some of us do and some of us don't.' 'Then let those who know tell those who don't', came the response. On the following Friday, the congregation decided they would not reply to his question at all. When no one answered his question, the jester looked in mock bewilderment all round the mosque. 'Dear me', said he, 'I am quite alone; nobody has come to mosque today.' And with these final words, he left, leaving the worshippers to do without his sermons.

One further story about this Turkish funnyman illustrates how free jesters were to criticize the society in which they lived—a luxury not afforded to more serious compatriots. Although he was not a very learned man, Nasr ed-Dîn was often called upon by citizens to give advice and settle disputes. On one occasion three men were quarrelling about their shares of a sack of walnuts. They could not agree and asked the jester to decide how the walnuts should be justly divided between them. Justice, however, was not enough; they wanted Nasr ed-Dîn to divide 'as Allah would divide'. He agreed, whereupon he gave one walnut to the first man, a handful to the second and the remainder of the sack to the third. Angrily they protested. 'O fools', said the jester 'when did Allah divide anything equally among men? As would Allah, so have I divided.'

Janice Gillespie, a truly feminine clown (*Colorific: photo by Don Hunstein*)

Modern street clowns have travelled a long way from the traditional auguste and white-face clown make-up, as this London busker demonstrates (*Daily Telegraph Colour Library: photo by John Sims*)

Davide of the Clown Cavalcade
troupe (*far left*) without make-up,
(*left*) applying the finishing touches
to his white-face clown mask and
(*below*) with disguise complete
(*Nick Birch*)

right: This clown's painted smile
hides a sad expression (*ZEFA:
photo by William L. Hamilton*)

An auguste wearing the strictly traditional colours of black and white (*Colour Library International*)

A white clown applying black squirls to a make-up that covers both face and neck. Some clowns cover only the face; these are known in America as dirt-necks (*Colour Library International*)

3 Court Jesters

The coat of arms of the eighteenth-century statesman Sir Robert Walpole bears the head of a man wearing a coronet from which emerges a jester's cap; the heraldic motto on the arms is: 'Speak what you think'. This motto could well have been adopted by all court jesters. From ancient times until the early seventeenth century, they entertained and amused with astonishing freedom of speech in the palaces of monarchs, the homes of wealthy families and churchmen and, later, in brothels and taverns.

As we have seen, the tradition of tolerating plain speaking from the jester may have originated in the primitive belief that fools and madmen were touched by divinity and that any indiscretion was either caused by ignorance or inspired by God. In a despotically-ruled society, those who dared to speak out against authority must surely, it was thought, be 'mad'. In old Russia a truly insane 'fool' had a better time of it; far from being locked up, fools enjoyed the confidence of the tsars, who often acted upon their advice. Significantly, Tolstoy speaks of the mentally deranged as 'God's people'.

The material advantages enjoyed by the court fool—splendid clothes, comfortable apartments, his own servants (in some cases, unfortunately, keepers)—were sufficiently attractive to induce many a sharp-witted man literally to play the fool. These 'artificial fools', or jesters, had official status by the fourteenth century and had taken the place of real fools in many royal households.

Unlike a real fool, of course, the jester could provide humour on demand, and was in the true tradition of clowning. He was ready to supply a witty phrase or a bit of horseplay when his master required it. Some of his jokes were extremely bawdy, but in those days royal courts had not acquired refined manners. Others may strike us as rather laboured, but they obviously went down well with their audience. In addition to providing entertainment for people who had no printed books and who, in most cases, could not have read them anyway, the jester served a purpose that was probably not recognized at the time but that we can now appreciate: he represented the principle of freedom of speech in an age in which such freedom hardly existed for anyone else.

There is a popular feeling that freedom of speech implies support of the poor and oppressed. But many jesters used their freedom purely in their own self-interest. Their closeness to the throne gave them considerable power, and like all powerful people they had enemies. Some people resented their immunity from censorship; others resented the favours they procured for their friends. Archy Armstrong, the Scottish jester to the Stuart kings James I and Charles I, seems to have been heartily disliked, except by his masters, and managed to incite many petty quarrels among the courtiers, while at the same time enriching himself enough to become a moneylender and landowner later on in his career.

above: Jesters from a thirteenth-
century manuscript (*BBC Hulton
Picture Library*)

right: A more modern version (*Mary
Evans Picture Library*)

Archy is thought to have been born in Cumberland, where he gained a reputation as a sheep-stealer before being appointed jester at an early age by James VI, then king only of Scotland. He followed the king on his accession to the throne of England and took part in the fooleries arranged to amuse the court. They seemed mainly to have consisted of rough horseplay.

James VI was fond of his jester and gave him a permanent place among his personal attendants. There are several stories which show Archy to have been an unpleasant mischief-maker. On one occasion he caused a quarrel between James and his eldest son Henry by suggesting that the young prince was more popular than his father. Friends of the prince, enraged by the jester's impertinence, took their revenge by lying in wait for him on several occasions and tossing him in a blanket.

Despite his unpopularity, Archy amassed a large fortune. He received gifts, not only from the king (who, in 1618, gave him a patent for making tobacco pipes), but also from all the king's friends, from people seeking the royal favour and from various boroughs. His dress was as rich as that of the courtiers.

Archy's avarice made no difference to his importance at court. John Taylor, the poet, dedicated a work of his to 'the bright eye-dazeling mirrour of mirth, adelanto of alacrity, the pump of pastime, spout of sport, and regent of ridiculous confabulations, Archibald Armestrong, alias the court Archy'.

Archy was included in the retinue of Prince Charles and the court favourite, the Duke of Buckingham, on their famous journey to Spain in 1623. James, encouraged by Buckingham, was hoping to bring peace to Europe by the marriage of his son Charles to the Spanish Infanta. Archy's career as a jester was then at its peak. He ingratiated himself with the Spanish royal family and won great favour from King Philip IV, after whom he named his son. Again he was showered with gifts and allowed to say what he pleased about the Spanish match —which despite his warm reception in Spain, was unfavourable. One of the English knights in attendance, Sir Toby Matthew, was so incensed by the jester's bluntness that he threatened him with hanging. Archy said to him, 'No one has ever heard of a fool being threatened for talking, but many dukes have been beheaded for their insolence'. Far from being intimidated, Archy continued his attacks upon the Spanish match, which was highly unpopular in England, and upon Buckingham.

The jester continued to hold his influential position when Charles became king. He was allowed as much licence and was just as generously treated, once receiving an Irish estate of 1,000 acres. So important had he become that godparents of his son included five of the highest officials and peeresses in the state.

The jealousy of the courtiers was bound eventually to cause his downfall. The fall from grace began when he upset Archbishop Laud by openly making fun of religious and political principles. When once he obtained permission to say grace at Whitehall in the Bishop's presence he cried, 'Great praise be given to God, and little *Laud* to the Devil'.

Not surprisingly, the archbishop was the cause of the jester's ultimate disgrace in 1637. News had reached the court of the rebellion at Stirling against Laud's attempt to impose the Book of Common Prayer on Scotland. As the archbishop was entering the council chamber on 11 March of that year Archy shouted to him: 'Whae's feule now? [who's a fool now?] Does not your grace hear the news from Striveling?'

The tyrannical Laud was so angered that he wanted Archy brought before the Star Chamber, but the jester's privilege saved him from this fate. Instead, he was merely banished from court and retired as a landowner to Arthuret, Cumberland, his probable birthplace.

On the frontispiece of the jest book attributed to Archy these words appear: 'Archee, by kings and princes graced of late, Jested himself into a fair estate'.

One other Stuart jester is worth mentioning, if only because he had the distinction of being only 18 inches tall. His name was Jeffery Hudson and he was born in Oakham—then in the county of Rutland—in 1619. His father, a strong man, was a butcher who kept and baited bulls for George Villiers, First Duke of Buckingham. At the tender age of nine, Jeffery Hudson was placed in the service of Charles I and Henrietta Maria, who had passed through Rutland and seen the jester perform at a dinner party given by Buckingham in their honour. The tiny lad was brought on to the table concealed in a pie from which he emerged to the great delight of the company. The queen was particularly amused and the jester passed into her service to become a court favourite.

Whereas Archy Armstrong was almost universally disliked, one of his predecessors won universal adoration. He was William Sommers, one of the jesters to Henry VIII. His picture hangs in Hampton Court Palace, and an admiring description of him appears in a book written by one of Shakespeare's actors, Robert Armin, entitled *A Nest of Ninnies* and published in 1608. Will is 'the poor man's friend', according to Armin, and 'one not meanly esteemed by the king for his merriment'.

Will Sommers born in Shropshire, as some say,
Was brought to Greenwich on a holy day,
Presented to the king; which fools disdain'd
To shake him by the hand, or else asham'd:
How er'e it was, an ancient people say,
With much adoe was wonne to it that day.
Lean he was, hollow eyde, as all report,
And stoop he did, too; yet in all the court
Few men were more belov'd then was this foole,
Whose merry prate kept with the king much rule.
When he was sad, the king and he would rime:
This Will exiled sadness many a time.
I could describe him as I did the rest,
But in my mind I do not think it best:
My reason this; how ere I do descry him,
So many knew him that I may belye him;
Therefore, to please all people, one by one,
I hold it best to let that paines alone;
Onely this much, hee was a poor man's friend
and helpt the widow often in the end.
The king would ever grant what he could crave,
For well he knew Will no exacting knave:
But whisht the king to doe good deeds great store,
Which caused the court to love him more and more.

Will was so loved that when he chanced to fall asleep on a stile in the park at Greenwich, rather than disturb him, passers-by walked round him. A woman who saw him asleep in this dangerous position placed a pillow beneath his head and tied him to the stile post with a rope to prevent him from falling. She stayed to watch over him until he awoke. The jester rewarded the woman by persuading the king to pardon her sons, who were to be hanged three days later for piracy.

Armin describes some of the riddles with which the jester would amuse the king. They were often of a somewhat coarse nature, as this example shows:

'Now tell me', quoth Will, 'if you can, what is it that, being born without life, head, lippe, or eye, yet doth run roaring through the world till it dye'. 'This is a wonder', quoth the king, 'and no question; I know it not'. 'Why', quoth Will, 'it is a fart'. At this the king laughed hartely and was exceeding merry.

Another method the jester used to amuse King Henry was to play practical jokes on Cardinal Wolsey, who could not abide Sommers.

Archy Armstrong (*left*) jester to King James I of England and (*right*) King Henry VIII's jester, William Sommers, here richly clothed, who was dubbed 'the poor man's friend' (*Mary Evans Picture Library*)

A story is told of how Will got the better of the powerful cardinal on an occasion when he dined with the king at Windsor. When Will entered the castle, he came upon a gathering of poor people at the gate. As he went into the presence of the king and his eminent guest, Will asked the king to lend him £10 to pay the cardinal's creditors, who had come for their money. The cardinal protested: 'I'll give your grace my head if any man can justly ask me a penny'.

Will, as usual, however, got his way and distributed the money to the poor waiting outside the castle. On his return the king asked who the creditors had been, the brewers or the bakers? Will replied that they had been neither and asked the cardinal to whom did he owe his soul. 'To God', came the reply. 'To whom thy wealth?' asked Will. 'To the poor', said the Cardinal. 'Take thy forfeit, Henry', said the jester. 'His head is thine, for to the poor at the gate I paid his debt, which he yields is due.' The king laughed merrily, but the cardinal's laughter was somewhat strained, since the high cost of the joke grieved him not a little.

Will Sommers was a very shrewd man as well as a master of wit. He was close enough to the king to be able to make comments on the abuses he saw about him

and warned Henry of the corruption of his treasury men. But in Armin's book he is more esteemed for his sheer kind-heartedness. Will's uncle is said to have visited Greenwich to complain to him of a recent enclosure by a Shropshire landlord named Tirrell of a common called The Firth. Sommers brought the grievance to the king's attention and caused the common to be reopened.

During Edward VI's reign Will retired from court. He is believed to have been buried at St Leonard's church, Shoreditch, on 15 June 1560.

One English jester must have had half of England in fits of laughter with his roistering, roguish, irreverent personality. This was John Scogan, jester to King Edward IV. He was unusual among jesters in being an Oxford scholar. His maxim was 'a merry heart doeth good, like a medicine'. Scogan's pranks may have caused much merriment, but not infrequently they involved some profit to himself. At Oxford—Oriel College, it is thought—he helped a simpleton son of a local husbandman into the priesthood for the bribe of a horse. One of his first jests when he arrived at the court of Edward IV was to stand under a water-spout during heavy rain, for the then enormous wager of £20. He won, but could very well have died as a result of the wetting.

Like most jesters Scogan was generously treated by his king. Edward gave him a house in Cheapside, London, as well as a country mansion near Bury St

44

Edmunds, Suffolk, thought to be the town from which he originally came. Scogan's wife was obviously conscious of the jester's wealth and social position and demanded of her husband that she should have a page to lead her to church, as was the custom among fashionable ladies. The jester affected sympathy and said that if she could not find her way to church alone she should have her page. He rose early on Sunday morning and chalked the road which lay between his house and the church gate. When the time came to set off for church, Scogan led his wife to see her new 'page'. No amount of wit on his part could assuage her fury.

Scogan played practical jokes on everyone, including his royal masters. The queen had asked to see Scogan's wife, whom she had never met, to ask her to influence her husband for good, since his raillery was becoming no laughing matter. Scogan did not improve things by misleading each woman into thinking that the other was deaf. The interview was pure farce.

Eventually Scogan went too far, and the exasperated king banished him to France. The joke which cost Scogan his comfortable position at court involved a large sum of money which he was said to have borrowed from the king. A day for repaying the debt had been arranged, but when the day arrived Scogan had no money. He decided the only escape from his liability was to fall sick and 'die'. He persuaded his friend to arrange his 'funeral' so that they would encounter the king en route. They entered into the joke with alacrity, and, wearing funeral clothes, carried off Scogan stretched out on a bier. In due course they came across Edward, who, very sad at the loss of his jester, made many kind remarks about him and said he forgave Scogan and his relatives the sum owed. On hearing this, the 'dead' jester leapt up, thanked his gracious creditor for his act of grace, and said, 'It is so revivifying that it has called me to life again'.

Exile did not have a chastening effect upon Scogan. He returned from France —without permission—with his shoes full of Picardy soil, claiming impunity on the grounds that he was not standing on English land.

In a book of Scogan's jests, compiled by a sixteenth-century physician, Dr Andrew Boorde, and published posthumously in 1626, we are told of a trick played by the jester on people of Normandy. It appears that Scogan approached a priest and confided that he had a relic of a head which had told him to raise money from the people to build a church. He promised the cleric half the proceeds if he would let the appeal be made in his church, and the greedy fellow agreed. When the congregation came to make their offerings, Scogan ensured their generosity by saying, 'All you women who have been faithless to your husbands, I pray you sit still, and come not to offer, for the head bade me that I should not receive your offerings.' Needless to say Scogan made a good deal of money from this exploit.

An English priest, who was not quite so lucky as the French one, was riding one day with Scogan and one of Scogan's friends, for churchmen loved the merry company of jesters as much as the less spiritual nobility. The jester, who, as usual, was short of cash, asked the priest if he should pray to God for funds. The priest replied that if he did so surely his prayers would be answered. Sadly the first attempt at bringing pennies from heaven achieved not a thing. Scogan then persuaded the priest to accompany him in his prayers, since he believed that might have more effect. But first he asked the priest how much money he had on him. Now the priest possessed £50, but he decided that in the circumstances it would be more prudent to admit to carrying only £5 with him. A second

The clown and jester Richard Tarlton was said to be among the few people who could 'undumpish' Queen Elizabeth I. He is seen here with his tabor as clown in *Henry V* (not Shakespeare's play of that name) (*BBC Hulton Picture Library*)

Jeffrey Hudson, the eighteen-inch high Stuart jester of Queen Henrietta Maria (*Mary Evans Picture Library*)

attempt was made to persuade God to relieve the poverty of the company. After about half an hour of devout worship, Scogan asked his companions to empty their pockets and purses to see if God had answered their prayers. Scogan emptied out the two shillings he had owned to begin with, but was delighted to see the bounty revealed by the priest. Grandly he returned the £5 which the priest had admitted to at the start and divided the remainder between himself and his friend, with their unwilling benefactor unable to protest.

Dr Boorde, who compiled Scogan's jests, agreed with the jester's view that mirth was good for the health. King Edward had died seven years before Boorde was born, so it is quite probable that the doctor heard the stories he set down from people who were young during Edward's reign. At the beginning of the *Scoggin's Jests* Boorde quotes a verse the jester made at Oxford on becoming a Master of Art:

> A master of art is not worth a fart
> Except he be in schools;
> A Bachelor of Law is not worth a straw
> Except he be among fools.

After returning to England, Scogan was eventually pardoned by the king. He died shortly afterwards of a 'perillous cough' and was buried, as was his wish, underneath one of the waterspouts of Westminster Abbey 'for I have ever loved a good drink, all the days of my life'. Death did not exactly put an end to Scogan's jests; references to them were plentiful throughout the sixteenth and seventeenth centuries.

Richard Tarlton, jester to Queen Elizabeth I, was a very different character from Scogan. He had a limited education, and, despite the patronage he received, was very poor. He ended his days in 1588 at the home of a woman of poor reputation after spending his last few years in dissipation in Shoreditch.

During his lifetime, however, Tarlton won enormous fame as a comic actor—more a star of the stage than a court jester. He was able to divert the temperamental Elizabeth when she was in her worst moods and was said to be among her 'highest favourites'. In all probability Tarlton served as a go-between for courtiers afraid to approach the queen themselves.

Tarlton, who was also a composer of ballads and a skilled fencer, had a head start when it came to making people laugh, for he had a particularly unprepossessing appearance, characterized by a flat nose and a tendency to squint. Like most good clowns, Tarlton had hardly to utter a word before his audience was amused. A contemporary writer says of him: 'The people began exceedingly to laugh when Tarlton first peept out his head.'

During the last five years of his life he won great popularity on the stage. He is believed to have played the part of Derrick, the clown in a pre-Shakespearian play about Henry V, and in 1583 he joined the newly-formed Queen's Men, soon to be one of the most famous theatrical companies of the day. Tarlton excelled at improvising doggerel verse on themes suggested by the audience—a practice that became known as Tarltonising. A book of Tarlton's jests was published in about 1600, but it makes surprisingly dull reading. His wit was apparently of the spontaneous kind that does not lend itself to the printed page. Hamlet's elegy on Yorick, recalling his 'gibes . . . gambols . . . songs' is said to have been inspired by Tarlton.

A nineteenth-century impression of Rahere, the jester to King Henry I of England, who became a prior and founded the priory and hospital of St Batholomew, London, the scene of the popular St Batholomew Fair (*Mansell Collection*)

One royal jester is best known for having founded a hospital. This was Rahere, jester to the English court of Henry I and his Queen, Matilda, in the early 1100s. Like his master, he was a Norman, and by all accounts he was a blithe but exceedingly cunning man. After he had danced, fiddled and jested for the amusement of the court for some years he grew tired of it all and went on a pilgrimage to Rome as penance for his philandering ways. While there, he became ill with malaria, and he vowed that if his life were spared he would build a hospital for the poor. Once recovered, he started home, and on the way he saw a vision 'full of dread and sweetness' in which the figure of St Bartholomew appeared. The saint told Rahere that he was to found a church 'in a suburb of

47

A nineteenth-century view of court jesters in an antechamber (*BBC Hulton Picture Library*)

London at Smedfeld' (Smithfield). And so the former jester built a great priory church—of which he was the first prior—and a hospital, both dedicated to St Bartholomew. The priory was later dissolved by Henry VIII, but the church is still in use today, and 'Bart's' Hospital, as it is familiarly known, is one of London's most renowned teaching hospitals.

Although few jesters can match Rahere's high-mindedness, there are stories of court fools who were extremely loyal to their masters and in some cases were responsible for saving their lives. A jester called Golet intervened to save the life of William, Duke of Normandy, in 1047. Hostile noblemen had conspired to kill the duke in his sleep. But the faithful Golet took hold of a stick which he used to bang upon the bedchamber door, shouting a loud warning to his master as he did so. The duke survived and subsequently became William the Conqueror of England.

A similar tale is told of the French jester, Chicot, but with one difference: Chicot's act of loyalty to Henry IV cost him his own life. Chicot was a particularly shrewd man and was very close to the king, to whom he gave political advice. Like Scogan he was of gentle birth; in addition, he had military training.

The jester was instrumental in persuading Henry of Navarre to become a Roman Catholic in order to be eligible for the French crown and so bring peace to a nation torn by religious strife. Chicot took an active part in the siege of Rouen in 1592, captured the Count of Chaligny and presented him to the king. But the count was so enraged at having being captured by a clown that he

Velasquez painted many dwarfs and jesters who entertained the royal families of seventeenth-century Europe, among them this portrait of the jester of Don Juan of Austria (*Mansell Collection*)

snatched back the sword he had surrendered and struck Chicot on the head. Jesting to the very end, Chicot died within two weeks.

The French kings were particularly fond of jesters. Charles V, 'The Wise' (1364-1380), kept several and even raised elaborate tombstones to their memory. An amusing story is told of Triboulet, the famous jester to Louis XII and Francis I, who was as simple-minded as Chicot was astute. His gift for mimicry, particularly of religious figures, and for music and dancing, seem to have been the reasons for his great popularity at the French court. On one occasion, however, the lord chamberlain was annoyed by Triboulet's too-exact imitation of his voice and sarcastic description of his character—which had greatly amused the company in the banqueting room. The angry chamberlain sought out the jester later and threatened to use his dagger to 'stop the loquacious folly for ever'. In traditional cowardly fashion, Triboulet fled to the king to ask his protection. 'Be of good cheer, merry cock', said the king, promising that if the chamberlain harmed a hair of the jester's head he would be hanged the next morning. This promise did not console the jester greatly. The day after would be too late, he said; 'he may thrust his knife between my ribs tomorrow; couldn't you hang him the day before?'

Similar French wit is displayed in this story of the splendidly dressed and pampered Maître Jehan, fool to Philip VI (1328-1350) and his successor, John II. Jehan was asked to intervene in a quarrel which had broken out in Paris between a street porter and the keeper of a cooked-food shop. The porter had sat himself down by the shop doorway so that the smell of the cooking meat drifting outside might make the plain bread he was eating taste a little more savoury. He was annoyed to find, however, that the shopkeeper greedily expected to charge him for this dubious privilege and a fight took place between the two. In an effort to bring about peace, Jehan made the solemn judgement that the porter should pay for the smell of the meat with the sound of his money!

Mathurine, a woman jester to Henry IV of France, was very strong minded, and her freely expressed views once almost landed her in trouble. A fanatical Roman Catholic, she often used her wit to ridicule the Huguenot faith, and the king knew that she suspected him of lukewarm devotion to his newly adopted religion. In 1594 she was accused of being an accomplice of Jean Chastel, who had wounded Henry in an attempt on the king's life. She did, however, manage to prove her innocence and was released from the dungeon into which she had been slung. Like a few other jesters, Mathurine used to assume madness for comic effect, and she would stalk the streets dressed as an amazon, followed by crowds of jeering children.

Political writers of the time who advocated a hard line against Protestants often used Mathurine's name as a pseudonym on their own writings. They also used that of Maître Guillaume, another jester with strongly orthodox views. He did not seem to have the need to pretend to madness; his eccentricity was very real. He would go abroad carrying a stick with which he would strike young boys, crying 'murder!' as he did so. It was his opinion that the cheeky little urchins had been created by the Devil while God was busy creating the angels. When Henry IV grew tired of his ministers' long and tedious speeches he would dismiss them by saying 'tell the rest to Maître Guillaume'.

Jesters were particularly popular among noble families in Italy, where, during the Renaissance, they enjoyed the fame now given to film stars. A favourite entertainment was to hear the jesters make fun of religion. Scocola, the favourite

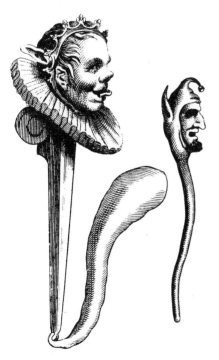

above: A German wood-cut by Karl Gehrts (*Mansell Collection*)

left: A selection of jesters' baubles, published in London in 1808 (*Mary Evans Picture Library*)

51

buffoon of Borso d'Este, preached a burlesque sermon in the streets; the money he collected he distributed among the poor. Like most jesters he was generously treated; he lived in his own home with his wife and large family and was granted the freedom of the city of Ferrara.

Another jester who amused by burlesquing church ceremonies and imitating friars was Il Matello, the eccentric servant of Isabella d'Este in the fifteenth century. The jester's real name was Bernadino, and he was a native of Quistello, in northern Italy. That jesters were passed around and sometimes exchanged is suggested by the story that in 1498 Isabella sent Il Matello to cheer up another member of her family, Alfonso, who had fallen very ill. The jester's visit was a great success. Alfonso wrote of Il Matello in enthusiastic terms and said that he had almost made him forget the severity of his illness. A year later Il Matello himself became ill—in his case, fatally. He was said to have behaved with great courage and acted the buffoon until the moment he died. Isabella honoured him by burying him in the family tomb, and with her family she sincerely mourned the jester's death. To them he was irreplaceable 'for nature had made him unique'. A sonnet was written on his death by a poet called Il Pistoia:

> Lifeless his body lies: if he is blest
> Even now, I think his parted soul let free
> Is making Paradise laugh heartily;
> But if he is in Hell, then, verily,
> He cheers a quiet Cerberus with a jest
> For Nature made of him so odd a fellow,
> So touched his brain even from his earliest year,
> That all who knew him called him Il Matello
> To both the Marquis and his wife most dear
> And not to them alone; all joyed to hear
> His jokes, whether in the country or the court,
> With him, even Death made sport,
> And during the transit, laughed with him awhile
> And then, still jesting, killed him with a smile.

We have already seen that jesters were well rewarded for their wit. In fact, like Scogan, they often used their wit to take advantage of the gullible and so enrich themselves. In addition to official fools, there were freelance jesters who often followed the courts on journeys and gained great riches en route. Even the serious intent of the Crusades did not stop the merry clowns from going along with the knights to bring them cheer. In the *Histoire des Croisades* by Jacques de Vitry (c. 1180-1240), Bishop of Acre, we read:

And it happened even more often that the nobles, having succumbed to extravagance and luxury, wasted a lot of money on their tournaments and their grand and worldly vanities, and got into debts with money-lenders, while clowns and jesters, vagrant parasites and actors, dogs of the court and flatterers plundered them of their inheritance.

Jesters were richly dressed. If there were several of them with their servants in one household, a strict pecking order made sure that the favourite was more expensively garbed than his servant or lesser colleagues. Much frenzied leaping

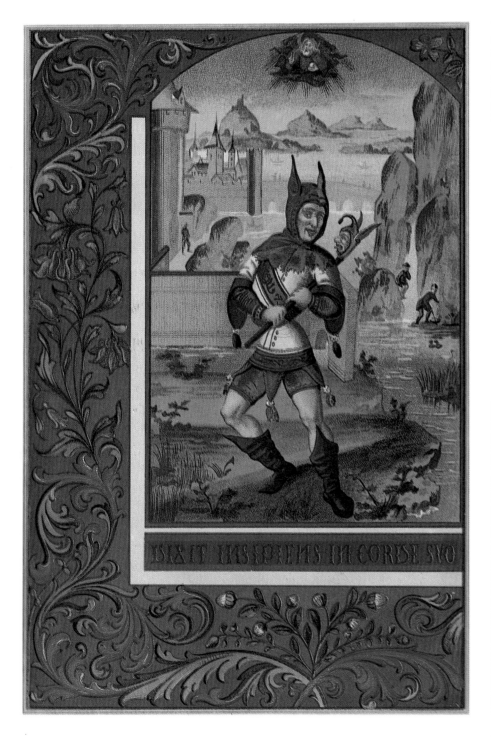

This court fool of the fifteenth century carries a bauble or fool's staff; his ornate motley suggests that he was well rewarded for his wit by his royal master. A facsimile of a miniature from a manuscript in the Bibliothèque de l'Arsenal (*Culver Pictures Inc*)

A theatrical scene on a Greek vase of 380 B.C. in the British Museum. Greeks loved to see their myths and heroes mocked by fools, and the particular scene depicted here is from the myth of the wise centaur Cheiron (*Michael Holford Library*)

left: This Flemish court scene shows a jester wearing imitation ass's ears attached to a cap in the shape of a fish tail. The picture is dated 1382, but asses' ears and other animal disguises were worn by fools centuries before (*Mary Evans Picture Library*)

Instead of a bauble—a staff bearing a model of a jester's head—some fools carried a stick with an inflated bladder attached to it, as these thirteenth-century merry-makers do. Their bare legs and poor clothing suggest that they did not enjoy the privileged, official status of some later court fools. The original illumination from which the figure in the foreground is taken represents a fool receiving a paper, probably a grant or benefit, from a king (*BBC Hulton Picture Library*)

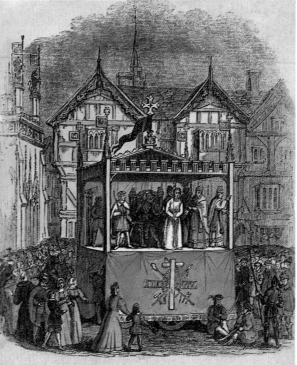

A performance of a Wakefield Mystery Play at Coventry. The Mysteries—religious plays on biblical themes, sometimes performed over a cycle of several days and staged by amateurs—provided a popular source of broad comedy (*Mansell Collection*)

Cap and bells are worn by jesters on this Munich picturesheet. The jester on the right thumbs his nose for the entertainment of two guests at a feast; the jester on the left enjoys a status that allows him to take part in a serious court function (*Mansell Collection*)

Christmas revels are enlivened by mummers—actors in disguise— seen frolicking here in a baronial hall, accompanied by minstrels in the gallery (*Mansell Collection*)

A French jester, with his cat (*Mary Evans Picture Library*)

about meant that a great many pairs of shoes were needed. Jesters were also provided with eared hoods, bells, swords and inflated bladders. Feathers and petticoats were sometimes worn.

The English monarchs were careful to provide for their jesters in old age. A feudal estate was awarded to William Piculph, the fool of Richard I, the Lionheart. Such generosity towards jesters did not always meet with approval. Thomas Lodge, the late sixteenth- early seventeenth-century writer, although against Puritan censorship of the theatre, warns against jesters, in a book entitled *Wits, Miserie, and the World's Madness:* 'Keep not this fellow company, for . . . your wardrobes shall be wasted, your credits cracked, your crowns consumed, and time, the most precious riches of the world, utterly lost'.

In amusing their employers jesters did not always rely on their own resources, however great. They often had recourse to the various jest books which were circulated.

Some of the stories were of eastern origin. One author was Poggio Bracciolini, a Florentine scholar and secretary to several popes in the fifteenth century, who produced a book of ribald tales. Other authors were the aforesaid Dr Boorde and Richard Tarlton, as well as John Bastell (1475-1536), a lawyer from Coventry and brother-in-law to Sir Thomas More, and Anthony Copley, who published a book of Spanish jests in 1574. The following examples taken from John Wardroper's recent anthology, give an idea of the kind of material used to entertain a king.

A drunkard passing over a bridge, his eyes so glared that he thought there were two bridges and stopping upon the wrong bridge, down he tumbled into the brook; where drinking his belly full of water, he continued saying, 'No more now, hostess, no more now'.

In a certain parish a friar preached, and in his sermon he rebuked them that rode on the Sunday, ever looking upon one man that was booted and spurred ready to ride. This man, perceiving that all the people noted him, suddenly half in anger answered the friar thus, 'Why preachest ye so much against them that ride on the Sunday? For Christ himself did ride on Palm Sunday. As thou knowest well, it is written in Holy Scripture'. To whom the friar suddenly answered and said thus, 'But I pray ye, what came thereof? Was he not hanged on the Friday after?' Which hearing, all the people in the church fell on laughing.

A man asked his neighbour, which was but late married to a widow, how he agreed with his wife, for he said that her first husband and she could never agree. 'By God', quod the other, 'we agree marvellous well'. 'I pray ye, how so?' 'Marry', quod the other, 'I shall tell ye. When I am merry, she is merry, and when I am sad, she is sad. For when I go out of my doors I am merry to go from her, and so is she. And when I come in again I am sad, and so is she'.

A valiant captain that had lost his leg formerly in the wars was nevertheless for his great prudence and courage made captain of a ship; and being in the midst of an engagement, a cannon bullet took of his wooden supporter so that he fell down. The seamen—forasmuch few knew he had a wooden leg—called out for the surgeon. 'The surgeon, a pox on you all!' said he. 'A carpenter! A carpenter!'

4 Medieval Merriment

The people of the Middle Ages had plenty of reasons for seeking the diversion offered by comical entertainers. Their lives were threatened and often cruelly shortened by the plague; most of them had barely enough to eat; they might at any moment be caught up in one of the innumerable wars waged by their lords, both temporal and spiritual; and any comfort offered by their religion was outweighed by its preoccupation with the Devil and eternal damnation.

It is small wonder that people flocked to fairs and delighted in feast day revels and wayside entertainment. Here they could forget the hardness of their lives in the enjoyment of tumblers, contortionists, jugglers, conjurors, bull- and bear-baiters and the jolly antics of the mummers and mystery players.

While kings laughed at their jesters and the common folk at fairground entertainers, the clergy, too, had their amusements. The early church had condemned all forms of entertainment, and some religious houses maintained an austere way of life, but in others the rules were considerably relaxed. They often rang with the sound of joyous singing, the music of harps and drunken laughter. Robert Grosseteste, the thirteenth-century Bishop of Lincoln, kept a harper, and some churches retained their own troupes of minstrels. Durham Priory engaged minstrels to perform at Christmas time and on St Cuthbert's Day and maintained a fool to entertain the monks.

Before the formation of the guilds the word 'minstrel' was applied both to the wandering buffoon and to the poet-musician. While the church disapproved of the former, it held in highest esteem the minstrels employed in the great houses who sang of the deeds of romantic heroes and the lives of saints, of love and virtue, of blood and battle. The long recitals were not a little tedious and the nobleman would encourage the minstrel to relieve their *longueurs* with juggling, tumbling and dancing. The Norman courts were thronged with tumblers, jugglers and the lowest type of buffoon. The tumbling was often done by women. Chaucer refers to them as *tombesteres*. In England an office of king's juggler was in existence until the time of Henry VIII. Berdic occupied this post during the reign of William the Conqueror and is mentioned in the Domesday Book. He headed an entire company of entertainers whose duties also included animal training. Bears, monkeys, apes and dogs were taught to dance and imitate human actions. The jugglers were often well rewarded for their comical skills. One tumbler received 20 shillings because he frequently fell from his horse while riding before Edward II, much to that monarch's amusement.

Inevitably, the romantic tales sung by the minstrels were parodied, and comic versions of these songs were taken up by bands of wandering minstrels. The songs were not only satirical but also earthy and often blasphemous. Apparently, these itinerant comics did not enjoy the licence granted to the court jester. A Norman minstrel named Luke de Barra made the mistake of ridiculing Henry I

above: Performing animals of the
thirteenth century, from *Pongin's
Dictionnaire du Théâtre* (*BBC
Hulton Picture Library*)

right: Performing bear, engraved
by Thomas Bewick (*BBC Hulton
Picture Library*)

of England in a song which he sang for some of Henry's enemies. Furious, the king had the minstrel captured and ordered that his eyes be put out. The poor man perished of the injuries he received in a frantic struggle with his torturers.

A particular feature of twelfth-century France was a type of wandering minstrel called a *goliard*—drawn, interestingly, from the church. The *goliards* were taken from the cathedral schools of the north. Instead of the austere life of a monastery, they chose the joys of the open road, and, although churchmen themselves, they were noted for thumbing their noses at contemporary society and its beliefs. For the *goliards* life was meant to be sybaritic. The church's threat of eternal damnation did not affect their carefree indulgence in wine, women and song. They sang of these, of spring, the joys of the tavern, the pleasures of youth and of love.

Unlike that of the court minstrel, the repertoire of the wandering minstrel was wide and included—besides ballad-singing—knife-throwing, leaping through hoops, magic, juggling, presenting performing asses and dogs, operating marionettes and imitating birds. They were also expected to engage in witty repartee. One can easily imagine with what alacrity weary travellers on Europe's rutty highways would gather round these early entertainers. Such travellers— and there were many—would include pilgrims, pardoners, wandering friars, peasants out of bond, messengers, workmen, outlaws and, of course, the ubiquitous pickpockets.

Another popular attraction for wayfarers was the mountebank, a quack doctor who exploited the simple by peddling useless herbs for the relief of sickness. In order to sell the dubious pills and ointments he had to offer, the mountebank would clamber on to a stage or bench and deliver a pompous speech which claimed, with scant regard for truth, untold miraculous cures. He would often use bogus 'foreign' languages to make himself sound more impressive and would display endorsements and scientific qualifications which his unwary audience did not question. Shakespeare speaks in no uncertain terms of these fraudulent fellows:

> As nimble jugglers deceive the eye,
> Disguised cheaters, prating mountebanks,
> And many such like libertines of sin.

Worcestershire mummers as seen through the eyes of Victorian painter Charles Cattermole (*Culver Pictures Inc*)

But if the mountebank was a charlatan he was also good value for people hungry for entertainment. He enticed his onlookers with a clownish partner, a zany, who went by a popular clown name of the time: Jack Pudding or Merry Andrew. An old ballad tells us: 'A mountebank without his fool, is in a sorrowful case'. First the zany would arrest attention by skilful displays of juggling and tumbling. Sometimes a trained monkey would be used to add to the fun. But once an audience had eagerly gathered round the booth, the real enjoyment began. The zany played the comic to the straight part of the mountebank. He would introduce his master in a mock address which had a nice line in exaggeration. Then, while the mountebank was extolling the so-called marvels of his wares, using the latest jokes and the wittiest of language, the zany would prance about pretending to all kinds of aches and pains. After receiving the medication he would affect to be cured, bound upright with a somersault, and thank the mountebank for his aid, with many a wry face and whimsical aside.

The pair would also perform farcical skits on tooth-pulling and doctoring, with the zany as patient. The dentist scene has been reproduced in some form or other in many later entertainments, notably the commedia dell'arte and the modern circus. The play between the straight man and his seemingly cloddish but cunning partner has been an enduring type of humour.

One of the most famous of all comic servants to a patent-medicine seller was Tabarin. Jean Salomon Tabarin was a seventeenth-century French clown who set up shop with a peddler named Mondor at one end of the Pont Neuf in Paris.

Edward Corbould's nineteenth-century view of Christmas mummers (*Mansell Collection*)

Mondor would announce all manner of remedies for unimaginable ills and Tabarin would amuse the audience by deliberate misunderstandings and plain insults. Their witty dialogue captivated all Paris. Their farces, which were collected in jest books and were particularly popular with aristocratic ladies, came to be known as *tabarinades*.

Another mountebank's zany who achieved fame was William Philips. He was once publicly flogged at St Bartholomew's Fair for speaking out against the government and was warned to hold his tongue. The next time he appeared at the fair he held up a tongue which he had purchased from a butcher. Everyone laughed at the comical way he had chosen to heed the warning.

Bartholomew Fair was one of the biggest of the great fairs held throughout England during religious festivals. This fair, which lasted three days, offered the greatest possible variety of entertainers. Here, among the quacks, clothiers and other traders, assorted mummers, morris dancers, puppeteers and prattling fools created a merry hubbub. Musicians played the pipes, horns, trumpets, tabor and hurdy-gurdy to accompany the tumblers, contortionists, stilt-walkers, jugglers and women dancing on swords. There were horse-races and curiosities, such as a hare who drummed on a tabor with his paws.

64

A nineteenth-century impression of mummers (*Mansell Collection*)

Mummers from the time of Edward III, from a manuscript in the Bodleian Library, Oxford (*BBC Hulton Picture Library*)

65

Like the church and priory to which it was attached, Bartholomew Fair had been founded by the jester Rahere and had received a royal charter. Merchants came from all over the known world to trade there—mainly in cloth, but their activities were eclipsed—in the eyes of the public at least—by those of the entertainers.

It was difficult for the church to maintain its stern attitude towards entertainers while its own religious houses patronized minstrels and fools. In addition to the regular festivities led by minstrels and musicians, a special feast was held at Christmastide. It was called the Feast of Fools and featured the burlesque crowning of a bishop. This strange performance provoked the disapproval of Bishop Grosseteste who, in 1236, described the feast as 'replete with vanity and foul with voluptuosity'.

The ceremony normally took place in a cathedral on one of the feast days following Christmas—usually either on the Feast of the Circumcision

(1 January) or on that of Epiphany (6 January). A vicar, canon or, in some places,
a boy, was crowned as bishop. He would be baptized with three buckets of foul
water while a noisy boisterous procession made its way through the nave. The
Feast of Fools was particularly popular in France, where, on the Feast of
Innocents (28 December), a choir boy was crowned bishop. He then gave a mock
sermon and celebrated mass. Wearing masks, the clergy entertained themselves
by dicing on the altar and reciting ribald verses, accompanied by indecent
gestures, singing and dancing. Germany, too, had its Feast of Fools, held on
Twelfth Night. Fools dressed in multi-coloured hooded cloaks trimmed with
bells would join in a carnival, indulging in quips, pranks and general horseplay.

With such irreverent activities taking place within its own portals the church
was forced to relax its stern position on other entertainers. Religious thinkers
began to feel that, after all, drama had a value as a way of driving home moral
teaching. Thomas Aquinas, the thirteenth-century Italian theologian, acknow-
ledged that dramatic performances afforded solace to mankind, and thus could be
sanctioned, so long as the actors behaved in a seemly manner.

Thus the church provided an environment in which the clown could flourish.
For the mystery and miracle plays which developed from the dramatic parts of
the church's rites contained a large element of buffoonery, as natural to medieval
audiences as the gargoyles on the fabric of the church itself.

A fools' morris dance, from *Ancient
Mysteries* by William Hone,
published in 1823 (*BBC Hulton
Picture Library*)

The subject of the mystery plays was the whole of man's biblical history,
beginning with the Creation and ending with the Day of Judgement. The
touching, homely language employed and the slapstick humour which enlivened
the story made them enormously popular, and in time they moved out of the
church and into the streets. The populace may have wanted to be edified, but
they also liked their edification sweetened with laughter. If Noah had a refractory wife who needed a beating before she would consent to enter the ark, so
much the better for merriment. If the shepherds' conversation was bawdy, the
more the audience was cheered. And the rich comic potential of an aged Joseph
who discovers his virgin bride is with child hardly needs explanation.

Although the Devil was included in the cast ostensibly to inspire fear of Hell,
he became the principal comic character. He and his merry gang of under-devils
enlivened long speeches with a variety of peculiar noises, strange gestures and
contortions of the body. The Devil wore a costume of leather, hair or black
cloth and a grotesque mask. The attendants who joined him in his fiendish
intrigues almost always wore masks. Sometimes these were adorned with rams'
horns, but more often they portrayed a human face with a crooked nose, pro-
jecting jaw and, for good measure, a big wart on the cheek.

By the fourteenth century the mystery plays were patronized by the craft
guilds or municipal authorities. The players performed on two-tiered wagons
called pageants which were moved from one part of a town to another. Occasionally the performances took place in a church or guildhall; more usually they
were given in the streets and market-places. The Coventry cycle of plays lasted
from four to six days and began at six o'clock in the morning. At York, the
players reported for duty at four-thirty and were fined if late. The mysteries
varied from region to region and were known and performed all over Europe.

opposite right: A seventeenth-century
droll performed in the Red Bull at
Clerkenwell, London. From
Kirkman's *The Wits, or Sport upon
Sport* (*Mary Evans Picture Library*)

Changling

Simpleton

Tu quoque

French Dancing Mr

Sr I Falstafe

Hostes

Clause

The Lord of Misrule leading
Christmas revels in Tudor England.
On the right is a jester waving his
staff and bladder. From a painting
by Charles Green, 1884 (*Mary
Evans Picture Library*)

The morality plays, which developed later, resembled the mystery plays in
having an inventive comic figure whose physical comedy recalled that of the
Devil, but they differed in containing a strong element of satire. The plays dealt
with the more abstract theme of the battle of vice and virtue for the soul of man.
Vice, or Iniquity, sporting a wooden dagger, took the place of the Devil as
villain and personified a sinful human quality such as Pride or Lust. The
character's disguise enabled him to criticize freely the follies of the day. One of
the more obvious targets for satire was the quack doctor. He is burlesqued in a
scene showing the buying of unguents at a stall to anoint Christ's body. The
drug peddler would be given a language of his own, part Latin and part dialect—
an attack on the pedlar's great facility for blinding his simple listeners with
science. This doctor-cum-vendor was a common comic type and in the Berlin
and Vienna morality plays he was helped by a comic servant. Tax gatherers,
lechers, shrews and unfaithful wives were also targets for satirical humour.

The Vice character used all the tricks of comedy: he would chatter in nonsense speech, delight in cross-purposes and misunderstandings, and exaggerate
the emotions of anguish as he was finally dragged off to the jaws of Hell riding
on the back of the Devil, who repeatedly attacked him with his wooden dagger.

Satirical wit was also the province of the secular strolling players who took
part in short farces called interludes. In one Dutch interlude we come across the
quack doctor once more in a scene which revolves round an elixir, sold to an
aged peasant with a frisky wife. The remedy is supposed to restore the old man's
potency. The magic potion is contained in a jar into which the hopeful husband

72

Harlequin, one of the familiar figures of the commedia dell'arte, the popular comedy that originated in Italy and that influenced comedy in France, England and other parts of Europe for two hundred years (*BBC Hulton Picture Library*)

above: Each character of the commedia dell'arte had a distinctive costume and face mask which changed during the comedy' existence. This is Pollicinella in 1800, wearing the loose peasant clothing and the halfmask with the hooked nose that gives us the origin of Punch, the hero of the English farcical puppet show, Punch and Judy (*Mary Evans Picture Library*)

right: Tom Eller, a popular English pantomimist of the nineteenth century, in the role of Harlequin (*Mary Evans Picture Library*)

left: The cowardly figure of Scaramouch, whose skirmishes with Harlequin always ended in a cudgelling from Harlequin's magic bat. He is shown here as he would have appeared in the mid-seventeenth century (*Mary Evans Picture Library*)

below: Arlecchino, the original Italian version of Harlequin, in 1671 (*Mary Evans Picture Library*)

above: Pantalone, the stock old man from Venice, as he appeared in the mid-sixteenth century. He was usually depicted as very thin and wearing tight breeches-cum-stockings. His character survives today in the butt of the clown in pantomime (*Mary Evans Picture Library*)

right: Women in the commedia dell'arte did not play such sharply defined characters as the male actors; the main requirements were that they should be beautiful and accomplished as musicians and singers. This is Arlequine in 1855 (*Mary Evans Picture Library*)

is told to blow. The foolish fellow fails to notice that the jar is filled with soot, and as he blows he becomes as black as night. Unaware of his new complexion, he goes eagerly to his wife who gives him a thorough beating for his trouble.

These short topical farces, which were called *soties* in France and *Fastnachsspiele* in Germany, were the work of amateurs who joined the fool societies which originated in the Middle Ages. In France these *sociétés joyeuses* went by such names as the Abbé des Foux, the Connards, the Basoche and the Enfants-sans-souci. They were set up by young men, often university students or law clerks, who assumed the character of the fool in order to criticize the abuses of church and state. They garbed themselves in jesters' motley in colours which had a certain significance for them. The yellow and green of the Parisian Enfants-sans-souci, for instance, stood for gaiety and youth.

The societies were organized into mock kingdoms, ruled by annually elected leaders with titles such as Abbé de Malgouverne, Prince des Sots or Mère-Folle. They flourished for several hundred years — as popular with the nobility at first, as with the peasantry. Their skills were in great demand for public entertainment, and the court summoned them to act farces and devise pageants and royal ceremonies, masquerades and folk dances. Satire and scandal were their stock-in-trade, and they were free to indulge in them. Their status as legal institutions did not dull the edge of their mockery of the state. The Connards from Rouen portrayed the suffering fortunes of the world at the hands of its rulers with a comic football game in which a globe served as a ball. Opponents in the game were a mock Emperor Charles V, Henry VIII, Pope Paul III and a clown. A favourite character in the Enfants-sans-souci, Nicolas Joubert, Sieur d'Angoulevent, poked fun at the legal system (with the approval of King Henry IV) as the hero of a series of absurd lawsuits—much to the delight of Parisians.

The fool societies also ridiculed the foibles of common people. In Dijon, the Infanterie Dijonnaise, ruled over by the Mère-Folle, revived the ancient game of *chevauchée*, in which any local person who had committed what was considered a social sin was made the butt of humour. A man who had married a widow, been beaten by his wife or who had become drunk was seated on an ass with his face turned towards the tail, and much fun was had at his expense.

Eventually, however, the actors' tendency to mock the church as well as the state got them into trouble. During the mid-1500s there was a clamp-down on the societies, and they were forced to expunge religious material from their performances. Deprived of much of their satirical force, they deteriorated into innocuous performers at carnivals and masquerades.

A popular entertainer in England and Scotland was a master of winter revels known as the Lord of Misrule. The term Abbot of Unreason was used in Scotland. He appeared towards the later part of the Middle Ages and his task was to oversee the theatrical entertainments that were part of the Yuletide celebrations in the houses of the great and wealthy, inns of court and some university colleges. The revels, which exceeded anything the church indulged in, would begin on 31 October, All Hallows Eve, and last until the day after the Feast of Purification, early in February. One English Lord of Misrule was George Ferrers, who, to cheer the young Prince Edward, son of Henry VIII, made his solemn entry into the court as a mock king emerging from a representation of the moon. He was accompanied by courtiers, jesters, prisoners, stocks and a gibbet. The king's jester, Will Sommers, was engaged with him in a mock fight. In Scotland, the office came to an end in 1555; in England, it had disappeared by the time of Charles II.

5 Harlequin and Company

We might be tempted to think that the hardship and insecurity of life in the Middle Ages—along with the grimmer aspects of medieval religion—gave people a special craving for the release of laughter. But Renaissance man, who lived in a comparatively open-minded and optimistic society, was equally addicted to comedy. In fact, it was Renaissance Italy that produced what is perhaps the most enduring form of comic theatre: the commedia dell'arte. For some 200 years the commedia dell'arte flourished, not only in Italy but elsewhere in Europe as well. Traces of it still exist in the entrées of the circus clown, in the English Punch and Judy show and in the pierrots who perform in end-of-pier entertainments.

The commedia dell'arte was, in fact, the comic theatre in which clowns as we know them first appeared. Improvisation was its most important characteristic. The actors had their instructions pinned up in the wings of the makeshift theatres in which they performed and were given a brief scenario within which they extemporized. Each of them played a stock character, who was a caricature of some Italian type found in a certain town or region. The most enduring of these characters are Harlequin, Columbine, Pantaloon, Scaramouche and Pierrot.

The comedian was very much responsible for the development of his own particular role and would make up his speeches as he went along. These were witty, allusive, often obscene, and given in dialect. But if the actor ran out of inspiration he could always fall back on the *lazzi*.

The *lazzi* were interpolated gags or stock business—devices, if you like—which linked various scenes. The word itself is thought to have come from the Italian word for 'action', *le azioni*, although it might instead come from *lacci*—'strings'—suggesting the strings of the plot. *Lazzi* might include rough-and-tumble slapstick sequences, crude practical jokes, or various means of tripping up other characters. They were collected into books and categorized as jokes, monologues, comical outbreaks of anger, joking marriage proposals and scenes of madness, fear and despair. There were the *lazzi* of joy, of falling asleep, and of justice—which usually meant the drawing of lots. Some *lazzi* were intended to delay the action of the play by using by-play and banter. So, although essentially the plays of the commedia dell'arte had no written dialogue, the *lazzi* served as a repertoire of improvised exchanges or stage 'business' which could be adapted to any situation.

The comedy appealed not only to the Italian countrymen, who loved to see their neighbours' foibles so hilariously portrayed, but also to noblemen and royalty, in whose palaces the companies of the commedia dell'arte were invited to play. The dukes of Ferrara and Mantua were noted patrons. In order to cater for the tastes of people of different social classes, speaking different dialects (and

opposite left: 'The frolic of my Lord of Misrule' (*BBC Hulton Picture Library*)

79

Scene from the comédie-italienne by Claude Gillot, a French artist born in Langres in 1673. Gillot, who died in Paris in 1722, painted actors who appeared in public places there (*BBC Hulton Picture Library*)

—as they travelled through Europe—different languages as well) the actors had to have a high degree of talent, imagination and intellect and a deep experience of life. To be a buffoon was not enough; a quick and ready wit, grace of expression and gesture, and political, social and psychological insight were needed, along with the accomplishments of dancing, music-making, mime and acrobatics.

The commedia dell'arte had great influence in France. The companies which settled there in the sixteenth and seventeenth centuries were known as the *comédie-italienne* and were much admired by Molière—who is said to have drawn some of his inspiration from it—and also by Marivaux. The Italian players shared a theatre with Molière for fourteen years until 1672. The first company of Italian players had been invited to Paris in 1571 as part of the celebrations of the marriage of Charles IX. The fashion spread rapidly to other European courts.

In England, Shakespeare is thought to have seen the stylish commedia dell'arte players, and his play *The Tempest* has a very similar plot to that of *Li Tre Satiri*, one of the pastoral scenari of the Italians. Later, the eighteenth-century actor John Rich, who billed himself as 'Lun' at the Lincoln's Inn Fields and Covent Garden Theatres, kept alive the character of Harlequin as a rascally figure who, through dance and dumb show, also figured as a magician and lover.

The origins of the commedia dell'arte have been traced by various writers to the Roman Atellan mimes, comic novels in north Italian vernacular of the fourteenth and fifteenth centuries, the antics of medieval jongleurs and the witty

80

repartee of Italian courtiers. We shall begin with a remarkably gifted man named Angelo Beolco—actor, writer, philosopher, poet and perhaps the most important of the original creators of the commedia dell'arte.

Beolco, a citizen of Padua, was also a landowner, occupied with managing his family estates; but from 1520 until his death in 1542 his hobby was acting. During the carnival season, mainly in Venice, he would appear as 'Il Ruzzante' ('the Gossip'), a shrewd, comic peasant. This character made his first appearance in a play written by Beolco himself. The dramatis personae consisted of the common folk of Padua, each of whom was given a different dialect. By this means, misunderstandings and characters at cross-purposes became part of the fun. Il Ruzzante himself was a complex amalgam of shrewdness, simplicity, meanness, cowardice and humour. His popularity with the public lay in the fact that he had true feelings that they could recognize and understand as well as comically naive notions. He made an art of long-windedness, humorously spinning out a point which he could have made in one sentence.

'Départ des Comédiens Italiens en 1697', engraved by L. Jacob from a painting by Watteau (*Mansell Collection*)

Scapino. Cap. Zerbino.

Pulliciniello. Sig.ª Lucretia.

Scaramucia. Fricasso.

above: Commedia dell'arte characters from etchings by J. Callot (1593-1635) and *(right)* the opening of the new theatre of Comédie Italienne in Paris after the death of Dominique Biancolelli in 1688; Colombine presents the mask and bat of Harlequin to the new actor of the part while, in the background, Biancolelli's widow mourns on her husband's tomb (*BBC Hulton Picture Library*)

At times, Beolco would take a rest from entertaining the public in Padua, Venice or Ferrara and perform for his patron, Alvise Cornaro. He gathered together a few friends and created parts for them within a comic framework. So emerged a whole family of characters created by skilled actors of varied backgrounds. Some of the players had been itinerant tumblers and mountebanks' boys; others were educated people with diverse accomplishments to their credit: knowledge of Latin or medicine, a gift for poetry or music. Ottavio, for instance, could play the flute, theorbo, harp, hautboy, psaltery, cymbals and the organ. Francesco Andreini, who directed as well as acted, also played every kind of musical instrument; in addition, he could speak French, Greek, Slav, Turkish and Italian as well as his native Pistoian dialect. Moreover, he was a poet and

above left: 'Phillips, the Merry
Andrew', published in 1792; (*above
right*) an early nineteenth century
(1812) Harlequin by D. Dighton;
and (*left*) John Rich as Harlequin in
1753 (*BBC Hulton Picture Library*)

83

above: Mr Blanchard as Pantaloon and (*right*) Harlequin bows—an etching by Claude Gillot (*BBC Hulton Picture Library*)

writer and could boast membership of the Spensierati of Florence, one of the literary societies founded in principal Italian cities.

Harlequin was one of the more dominating roles of the commedia dell'arte. He was one of two *zanni* or comic servants, originally natives of the town of Bergamo. The word *zanni* is thought to come from 'Gianni', a diminutive of Giovanni. Harlequin was a simpleton, but a crafty, roguish one, whose slow wit was occasionally brightened with displays of shrewdness and clownish, ribald mockery. Although much of his comic appeal lay in his genius for parody and mastery of disguise, it lay mainly in the classic situation of the booby who is outwitted by a sharper-brained partner. Harlequin was supposedly a citizen of

84

the lower town of Bergamo, which was said to produce dullards, while Brighella, his partner, came from the upper town, where nimble wits were allegedly the rule.

Harlequin was particularly proficient at acrobatics and tumbling, a rubbery figure who has been likened by the theatre historian Pierre Louis Duchartre to a dolphin: 'The droll and whimsical . . . gliding, supple and black Harlequin makes one think of a dolphin, appearing and disappearing in the sea, bounding, turning and capering. He is always volatile and elusive.'

Along with his somewhat tyrannical and cruel crony Brighella, Harlequin plays his part in the romantic intrigues involving lovers, rivals and protective parents that form the basis for many of the comedy's plots. His task in the action is to lift heavy weights, spy, please, jest and sing. The character wears a mysterious mask featuring quizzically-shaped eyebrows, a beard and a wart on the cheek. His colourful diamond-patterned costume is well known. He wears a double-pointed hat and sometimes an animal's tail.

Commedia dell'arte performers often handed their parts down to their sons and daughters; sometimes Harlequin married his Columbine in real life as well as in make-believe. All of this helped to strengthen the harmony of the performance. Dominique, one of the best-known exponents of Harlequin in the seventeenth century, particularly in France, was the son of commedia dell'arte actors. His full name was Giuseppe Dominique Biancolleli.

This brilliant actor was well-built, agile and supple. He was clever enough to know how to turn even his defects to advantage, as do all true clowns. His particular shortcoming was a somewhat sharp, parrot-like voice. In time, however, the public came to accept his voice and refused to acknowledge a Harlequin with a voice unlike it. In France his voice was irrelevant; Spanish was a more popular language than Italian there at the time, and so the actor developed as a superlative mime, supplementing this with his athletic skill as a dancer.

Italian comedy players cavort in the street to entertain the populace (*Mansell Collection*)

Dominique arrived in France in 1654 after Mazarin, the Italian-born French cardinal and statesman, had asked him to join the Italian company in Paris. At the time, he was playing in Vienna with Tabarini's troupe. With him to Paris he took Ottavio, the foremost musician of the company, and others. Louis XIV found Dominique's famous wit most endearing. On one occasion, as the king was sitting at dinner, about to consume a dish of partridges, he noticed Dominique staring longingly at the game birds on his plate. Touched, the king said, 'Let Dominique be given this dish'. Instantly, Dominique replied, 'And the partridges, too?' The king agreed, much amused—a generous act indeed, for the dish was made of pure gold.

Despite the actor's superb skill as a mime, his company only really enjoyed success when performances were given in French. The troupe's popularity became well established—so much so that the strong competition it repre-

86

The Pierrots at Scarborough, Yorkshire, in August 1907 (*BBC Hulton Picture Library*)

sented aroused the resentment of the French comedians. Led by Baron, the comedians made a complaint to the king, hoping he would restrict the company's spoken drama. Louis refused to take action until he had heard from Dominique. Duly the actor arrived into the presence of the king and said to him, 'Sire, in what language shall I address Your Majesty?'

'Speak in any way thou wilt', replied the king.

The actor chose to interpret this as royal approval of his performing in French, and his company continued as before, to much acclaim.

There must be many stories of the sad clown. One about Dominique is very similar to one told at a later date of Grimaldi. Apparently, feeling very depressed, Dominique paid a visit to an eminent doctor. The doctor did not recognize the grieved face of his famous patient and declared that the simplest remedy for his ills was to go to see Dominique play in the comedy.

Like Grimaldi, Dominique died an early death as a result of his strenuous exertions. He was only forty-eight, and had just given a spirited parody of the royal dancing master and ballet composer. His death was sadly mourned; the theatre where he had played closed for an entire month as a sign of grief.

His twelve children followed in his footsteps, playing many stock roles in the commedia dell'arte. One of them was a godchild of Louis XIV.

Another famous Harlequin was an adroit actor known as Thomassi. He was born at Vicenza in about 1683, and at an early age he joined a troupe of actors touring Italy. He became a much-loved figure in both Italy and France and was renowned for his physical skill. His Harlequin, when faced with a threat, might

escape by turning a back somersault, at the same time holding a glass of wine
without spilling a drop. Thomassi's acting ability was no less remarkable; he
could bring tears of sorrow to the eyes of his audience just as easily as he could
make them roar with laughter—despite wearing the half mask of the commedia
dell'arte player. He died in 1739.

Pedrolino, the stock character from whom the later French Pierrot derives,
was a comic valet like the other *zanni*, but with a difference: he was less roguish
and certainly more personable. This charm was developed fully by the French
actor Jean-Gaspard Deburau. The Italian character appeared in the late
sixteenth century and was revived by the actor Giratone in the early seventeenth
century. Although tender and sensitive, Pedrolino became more naive and
awkward as time went on. When he joins Harlequin in playing tricks on the
doctor or Pantalone, it is he who gets caught and punished. His baggy costume
with exaggerated buttons is now universally familiar as that of the white clown.
He wore no mask and his face was heavily powdered.

The forerunner of today's Punch was a bumpkin called Pulcinella, a low
comedy clown who specialized in imitating animal noises. He grew to rival
Harlequin in importance, but began as a slightly hump-backed, pot-bellied
fellow, with puffy cheeks and an enormous mouth who got his laughs by his

above, right and *opposite right:* Actors of the Théâtre du Soleil, Paris, in a performance of *L'Age d'Or*, wearing the traditional leather half-masks of the commedia dell'arte (*John Topham Picture Library*)

slow, deliberate movement and a squeaky hen-like voice. The character originally became popular in the towns of Benevento and Naples; his popularity grew in Naples, where his country slowness was relieved by witty phrases, showing that he simply pretended to be stupid as a weapon of defence. In his carefree way, Pulcinella was unscrupulous and cruel; he was also coarse and might be found greedily eating his way through a pile of macaroni heaped in a chamber pot.

He wore a loose white blouse with a belt for carrying his purse and wooden sword. A scarf edged with green lace was knotted at his neck and on his head he generally wore either a skull-cap or a grey hat with an upturned brim. In Naples, however, he wore a black or white conical hat and exaggerated flowing pantaloons. In France, where he was known more as a blockhead than as a wit, Pulcinella wore striped stockings, and was endowed with the humpback and mask with huge protruding nose so familiar in today's Punch and Judy shows.

Towards the end of the seventeenth century Pulcinella found his way to England, where he gave full rein to the heartless excesses which were in his nature. Unlike the other *zanni*, he had a wife, whom he subjected to hateful domestic tyranny. The early adventures of Punch and Judy would certainly arouse the wrath of today's self-styled protectors of our morality. In them, the clown seduces a young girl, by whom he has a child, and goes on to take a mistress. Imprudently, his wife complains, at which Punch cleaves her head in two and tosses the infant from the window. He slays his parents-in-law and makes good his escape, seducing young women as he departs. Even the Devil is on the receiving end of Punch's cudgel. The law catches up with him and he is sentenced to be hanged. But Punch outwits everybody and finally hangs his executioner.

The first Pulcinella is thought to have been created by Silvio Fiorillo, an actor who ran a company of his own in his birthplace of Naples, towards the end of the sixteenth century. He appeared later with other companies and was the author of several plays and plots (*scenari*) in the commedia dell'arte tradition.

It was Tiberio Fiorillo (probably no relation to Silvio) who created the figure of Scaramuccia (Scaramouch), one of the boastful captains of the commedia dell'arte. Until the time of Tiberio, the captain parts were played with masks; however, this actor merely powdered his face instead and became known as 'the prince of grimaces'. Scaramuccia's splendidly dressed figure weaves his way through complicated intrigues involving numerous women, in which Pulcinella is his only ally. His skirmishes never leave him at a disadvantage; blows meant for him fall on innocent onlookers.

Tiberio Fiorillo, appropriately enough, was the son of a cavalry captain. The actor had led rather a racy life before he joined a small theatrical troupe. He took his Scaramuccia to Fano, near San Marino, where he scored great popular success, and with his company he then travelled to Mantua, where his acting attracted the attention of its duke.

Among his many gifts were a superb voice (he sang to his own lute accompaniment) and great skill as a dancer and acrobat. Even in extreme old age he was strong, agile and graceful. It was said that at the age of eighty he could raise his foot high enough to tap it on another man's face. Like Dominique, he was invited to the French court by Mazarin. Among his admirers were Anne of Austria, widow of Louis XII, and her illustrious son Louis XIV. Such was his popularity among the fashionable that one of his five children was baptized by a representative of the pope.

Tiberio became extremely prosperous; his possessions included a magnificent estate in Florence. A prince who saw him perform once in Rome remarked, 'Scaramuccia does not speak, but he says a great deal', and promptly made him a present of a coach and six horses.

London was graced by several visits from Tiberio Fiorillo, notably in 1673, when he became the darling of high society, who deserted their erstwhile favourites—French puppets and English actors—and flocked to see him perform.

This gifted clown, who could make audiences rock with mirth simply by the play of his features, died at about the age of eighty-five on 8 December 1694.

The character of Captain Scaramuccia, which Fiorillo helped to create, provided the actors with a chance to satirize Spanish adventurers who had followed the Emperor Charles V into Italy in the sixteenth century and overrun the cities of Naples and Milan. One unfortunate actor was beaten to death by Spanish officials for his lampoon of the alien soldier. Many different captains swaggered through the commedia dell'arte performances. Scaramuccia, or Scaramouch, is one of the best known. Another is Captain Spavento dell Vall' Inferno. In the hands of his creator, Francesco Andreini, this captain was not only an extravagant braggart but also a man who loved to show off his learning as well as his so-called courage. Andreini had undergone active military service, and for a year had been a prisoner of the Turks on a galley, so he was well-fitted to create his part of the absurd Spavento. In one scenario Spavento refuses to fight because he claims the soft blood of the Bolognese would cause his sword to go limp.

The Italians of the sixteenth century—like audiences of earlier times—were greatly amused by foolish, querulous old men. In the commedia dell'arte this species was represented by Il Dottore, from Bologna, and Pantalone, a self-important merchant created in Venice. The scraggy Pantalone, with his billowing black cape, his Turkish slippers, long red woollen stockings and red bonnet, was a well-known figure all over Europe. Historians have found a parallel between this foolish but authoritarian figure and the Pappus of ancient Roman mime plays. Pantalone hides behind a grotesque mask which has a prominent

Il Dottore Baloardo, the second of the two stock characters of the commedia dell'arte who embodied foolish, easily outwitted old men. Notice the large handkerchief slung around the belt so that it will be within easy reach during the emotional scenes. His garb is that of men of learning and science in Bologna in the mid-seventeenth century (*Mary Evans Picture Library*)

opposite above: Feste the jester charms Viola with wit and music in a Royal Shakespeare Theatre production of *Twelfth Night*, and (*opposite below*) he entertains the court of Duke Orsino with an 'old and antique song' (*Holte Photographics, Stratford-upon-Avon*)

'Joey' the Clown as he originally appeared; the frills and furbelows worn here by Joseph Grimaldi are a direct satire on the eighteenth-century dandy (*Mary Evans Picture Library*)

Grimaldi at the Sadler's Wells Theatre (*Mary Evans Picture Library*)

hooked nose, grey moustache and long, sparse beard. Round his waist is slung a pouch, a dagger and a handkerchief, which figures prominently in touching reunion scenes. Occasionally he is seen in round spectacles. Shakespeare knew of him and describes him in *As You Like It*:

> The sixth age shifts into the lean and slippered pantaloon,
> With spectacles on nose and pouch on side,
> His youthful hose well sav'd, a world too wide
> For his shrunk sack; and his big manly voice,
> Turning again towards childish treble, pipes
> And whistles in his sound.

In the 700 or so commedia dell'arte *scenari* which are extant, Pantalone plays many roles: he is sometimes married with a bunch of children who torment him by eloping or disappearing in other ways; he may even be a rival to his own son for the love of a pretty girl. He is often miserly and so mean that on one occasion he asks one of the *zanni* to buy him an egg which contains a chicken so that it can be used to make an omelette and a nourishing broth at the same time. Although he thinks of himself as wise and is fond of giving tedious advice and rebukes, he is a particularly credulous character and the butt of all the deceits and tricks of the *zanni* and of his children, who regard him with contempt.

Pantalone's counterpart from Bologna was the character of the doctor, for centuries a comic figure. Like the self-important merchant, the doctor is a miser, and given to long boring monologues to show off the learning of which he is inordinately proud and which sends his patients to sleep while they are waiting for his assistance. The doctor is dressed in a caricature of the normal clothing worn by men of sciences and letters in contemporary Bologna. The costume includes a long, ankle-length gown and small narrow-brimmed hat decorated with a plume, all in black. His half-mask is sometimes black and sometimes flesh-coloured. The doctor's cheeks are smeared with red to suggest his fondness for drink.

The fact that female roles were not so fully developed as the male characters in the Italian comedy is partly because before the Renaissance the church forbade women to appear on the stage. In the earlier stages of the development of the commedia dell'arte, as in Elizabethan theatre, boys played the parts of women. Later, the Italians helped to establish the use of women in female roles. The French saw women on the stage for the first time when the Italian comedy took that country by storm. The comediennes of the commedia dell'arte had to be as highly talented as the male actors. They were expected to possess great beauty and a good voice and to be able to dance and play musical instruments. The upper-class women characters wore costumes, embellished with gold and silver embroidery and with jewels. So as not to conceal their loveliness, the women of the commedia dell'arte wore no masks. They played the parts of comic maids, courtesans, sweethearts, mistresses—always involved in some romantic intrigue.

The commedia dell'arte is important in two ways. For one thing, it marked the first appearance in Europe of companies of professional actors, and it was a landmark in the history of clowning. The comic turns, rapid-fire repartee and practical jokes engaged in by the *zanni* and other stock characters provide the traditions of modern clowns and their entrées. It was a style of comedy that appealed to people of the day, whatever their language or nationality and which has come down to us through the centuries spreading universal gaiety, a carefree joy.

6 Shakespeare's Wise Fools

Unlike the *zanni* of the commedia dell'arte the clowns of Shakespeare are not types but individuals, whose function it is to comment critically upon the action of the play. The clown may not be essential to the plot, but he does provide a particular spirit and tone without which the play would seem incomplete.

Shakespeare probably drew some of his inspiration for his clowns from the mocking, malicious Vice character in the medieval interludes. But Shakespeare's clown is more genial; he makes fun of and highlights the affectation and folly of human beings, but with a warm, human touch which aids our insight into the behaviour of the more serious characters. The comic Vice laughed at failure to achieve the ideal; Shakespeare's clowns are concerned with the recognition of reality. They were the first wise fools to prance across the Elizabethan stage; their voice, the reasonable one of common sense.

Besides having a dramatic function, clowns were something of a theatrical expedient. For audiences, as Shakespeare well knew, flocked to the theatre to see not only the fine acting of Burbage and his rival Alleyn but also the clowning of William Kempe and Robert Armin.

William Kempe was particularly admired for his performances of jigs. Like the Italian comedy players, Elizabethan actors had to be accomplished dancers and singers, and occasionally instrumentalists. Music and dance figured prominently in the plays, and a favourite form was the jig, which was a dance with a sung dialogue.

Kempe, the original Dogberry, was more a low comedy clown than Armin, whose subtlety is reflected in the personages of Touchstone, Feste and Lear's fool. Both men were in the habit of improvising, and their ad-lib comments may well have been included later in the script. It was perhaps this extemporizing which prompted Hamlet to say to the players, 'Let those that play your fools speak no more than is set down for them'.

Armin, whose book *Nest of Ninnies* was referred to in Chapter 3, was the adopted son of the jester Richard Tarlton. Tarlton was a noted interpreter of the comic Vice character and a composer of jigs. It must have been from Tarlton, in part, that Armin acquired his clown's stock-in-trade: the clever logic-chopping that transcended mere buffoonery; the humorous twisting of well-known sayings; the bawdy, satirical and trenchant observations wrapped up in clownish prattle and slapstick.

Armin was very conscious of his ability as a clown. In his book *Phantasma, the Italian Tailor and his Boy* (1609), he refers to his 'constableship' and to having been 'writ down as an ass in his time'—very likely alluding to the fact that in his time he, like Kempe, had played the part of Dogberry.

The Dogberry role, in *Much Ado About Nothing*, is not as important as the court fools in other plays. Dogberry is a constable who sets the watch that

William Kempe, one of Shakespeare's clowns in the 1590s, dances a morris from London to Norwich in 1600. From the title-page of his *Nine Daies Wonder* (*Mander & Mitchenson Theatre Collection*)

captures Borachio and Conrade, examines them, but is dubbed an ass for his trouble. Dogberry would have been a country bumpkin type of clown, as opposed to a professional fool, and would speak with a country burr which at the time was known as 'Cotswold speech'. The more important fools in Shakespeare's plays were court fools and would wear the jester's motley to distinguish themselves from the slow-witted yokel clown, who would be recognized by his russet peasant clothing.

Although jesters had unlimited freedom to speak their minds, the customs of the court had still to be upheld, and it would not have done for a fool to appear too intelligent, as if on an equal footing with his master. A large amount of condescension was accepted by the court fool. Away from the court, the jester may have had rather more licence. In *As You Like It*, Touchstone, court fool to Frederick, the duke's brother, accompanies Celia and Rosalind into the pastoral loveliness of the Forest of Arden. There he can afford to parody courtly manners and freely ventilate his view of the banished lords in their leafy greenwood with an ironic scepticism. At one point Touchstone parodies courtly protocol in his recollection of a quarrel with a courtier:

> I did dislike the cut of a certain captain's beard. He sent me word, if I said his beard was not cut well, he was in the mind it was. This is called the Retort Courteous. If I sent him word again, it was not well cut, he would send me word he cut it to please himself. This is called the Quip Modest. If again, it was not well cut, he disabled my judgement. This is called the Reply Churlish. If again, it was not well cut, he would answer I spake not true. This is called the Reproof Valiant. If again, it was not well cut, he would say, I lie. This is called the Countercheck Quarrelsome; and so to the Lie Circumstantial and the Lie Direct.

Touchstone's view of the pretentious and modishly melancholy Jaques is all too clear in this parody of his trite philosophizing:

> It is ten o'clock;
> Thus may we see . . . how the world wags:
> 'Tis but an hour ago since it was nine,
> And after one hour more 'twill be eleven;
> And so, from hour to hour we ripe and ripe,
> And then from hour to hour we rot and rot,
> And thereby hangs a tale.

Jaques, unaware that he is the butt of the joke, applauds the jester, claiming that 'motley's the only wear'.

The Forest of Arden, which the characters extol for its simplicity, is not, as Shakespeare knows, without its drawbacks. He tells us this through the realistic eyes of Touchstone, who sorely misses the comforts of the court and who here compares the shepherd's life with the luxury he has left behind him:

> . . . in respect of itself, it is a good life; but in respect that it is a shepherd's life it is naught. In respect that it is solitary, I like it very well; but in respect that it is private, it is a very vile life. Now, in respect it is in the fields, it pleaseth me well; but in respect it is not in the court, it is tedious. As it is a

spare life, look you, it fits my humour well; but as there is no more plenty in it, it goes much against my stomach.

Even Touchstone's wooing of the rustic Audrey is a comment on the extravagant loves of the nymphs and shepherds, lords and ladies who surround him. Not for him the fine speeches and romantic pretensions; he has a worldly, hard-headed view of marriage: 'As the ox his bow, sir, the horse his curb, and the falcon her bells, so man hath his desires; and as pigeons bill, so wedlock would be nibbling.' He describes his Audrey as 'a poor virgin, sir, an ill-favoured thing, sir, but mine own'. This hardly echoes the conventions of romantic, pastoral love. He laughs at love's illusions, and his description of his courtship of the dairymaid Jane Smile sums up the whole play in the realistic, though genial,

above: Shakespearian clown Robert Armin as he appeared on the title-page of his own play *Two Maids of Moreclacke*, produced by the King's Revels in 1609 (*Mary Evans Picture Library*); *left:* Dogberry in a scene from *Much Ado About Nothing* (*Mansell Collection*)

101

eyes of the clown: 'as all is mortal in nature, so is all nature in love mortal in folly.'

Touchstone, as his name implies, is at the centre of the play. He is not absolutely necessary to the plot, but without his rich honesty the silly, self-conscious pastoral affectations of the lovers would not be put into perspective. He was the first truly wise fool on the Elizabethan stage. The part was written for Armin, who replaced Kempe as the chief comedy actor in the *Lord Chamberlain's Men* in about 1599.

Another clown part which Shakespeare wrote for Armin was Feste in *Twelfth Night*. Feste has a great deal in common with Touchstone; again the character is not essential to the plot and again his wit is used to show to the audience the foolishness of the other characters, who live in the dream world of Illyria. Feste, too, is a court jester, an 'allowed fool'. Unlike Touchstone, Feste is a musical role; the clown sings several charming songs in the play, including the well-

above: Touchstone in a 1775 production of *As You Like It* (*Mary Evans Picture Library*) and (*right*) Touchstone and his homely Audrey as played by Mrs. H. Marston and Mr F. Younge (*Mansell Collection*)

known 'O Mistress mine!'. Feste is ironical, witty and wise, and it is his perception that points to the absurdities of Olivia's mourning, the Duke's melancholy fascination with the idea of love and the splendidly comic self-love of Malvolio.

When the sentimental Olivia grieves for a brother dead for seven years, Feste teases her:

Clown: Good madonna, why mournest thou?
Olivia: Good fool, for my brother's death.
Clown: I think his soul is in hell, madonna.
Olivia: I know his soul is in heaven, fool.
Clown: The more fool, madonna, to mourn for your brother's soul being in heaven. Take away the fool, gentlemen.

Feste is no less hard on the Duke:

Now the melancholy god protect thee, and the tailor make thy doublet of changeable taffeta, for thy mind is very opal! I would have men of such constancy put to sea, that their business might be everything and their intent everywhere; for that's it that always makes a good voyage of nothing.

At one point he joins the plot of the play by entering into the light-hearted conspiracy against Malvolio. He pretends to be a curate, Sir Topas, and in a display of bogus esoteric learning we hear an echo of the mock sermons so beloved of the continental fool societies:

Mal: I am not mad, Sir Topas, I say to you this house is dark.
Clown: Madman, thou errest: I say, there is no darkness but ignorance, in which thou art more puzzled than the Egyptians in their fog.
Mal: I say this house is as dark as ignorance, though ignorance were as dark as hell; and I say, there was never man thus abused. I am no more made than you are: make the trial of it in any constant question.
Clown: What is the opinion of Pythagoras concerning wild fowl?
Mal: That the soul of our grandam might haply inhabit a bird.
Clown: What thinkest thou of this opinion?
Mal: I think nobly of the soul, and no way approve of his opinion.
Clown: Fare thee well: remain thou still in darkness: thou shalt hold then opinion of Pythagoras ere I will allow of thy wits, and fear to kill a woodcock, lest thou dispossess the soul of thy grandam.

It is in the same scene that Feste refers to his ancestry, the comic Vice:

> I am gone, sir,
> And anon, sir,
> I'll be with you again,
> In a trice,
> Like to the old Vice,
> Your need to sustain;
> Who with dagger of lath,
> In his rage and his wrath,
> Cries, 'Ah, ha'! to the devil . . .

There is no question that Feste's superiority is as much recognized by the characters in the play as by himself. He is not too happy at being taken for a fool and describes himself as Olivia's 'corrupter of words'. Malvolio dubs him a 'barren rascal' and Viola commends him:

> This fellow is wise enough to play the fool,
> And to do that well craves a kind of wit.

Feste's humour is less indecent than that of the other fools, although Eric Partridge in his study of 'Shakespeare's Bawdy' suggests that the closing song of *Twelfth Night*, 'When I was and a little tiny boy', sung by Feste, summarizes a lifetime's sexual experience. Jokes about sex and other indelicate subjects are more the province of Lavache, the leering jester in *All's Well That Ends Well*.

Lavache does not bring to the play the insight of Feste or Touchstone. He is more akin to other Elizabethan stage fools, typically sardonic and wilful; in the words of the Duke of Florence, 'he has no pace, but runs where he will'. But he does have a touch of reality and human warmth; as is evident in the reason he gives for wanting to marry his Isabel:

> My poor body, madam, requires it: I am driven on by the flesh; and he must needs go that the devil drives.

Two scenes from *Twelfth Night*: (*left*) Sir Andrew Aguecheek, Feste the clown, Sir Toby Belch and Maria (*BBC Hulton Picture Library*) and (*below*) the same characters interrupted by Malvolio in a performance given at Stratford-upon-Avon in 1864 (*Mary Evans Picture Library*)

Lavache makes us laugh by his skilful word-play and, in particular, by his ridiculous similes:

Countess: Marry, that's a bountiful answer that fits all questions.
Clown: It is like a barber's chair that fits all buttocks; the pin-buttock, the quatch buttock, the brawn-buttock, or any buttock.
Countess: Will your answer serve fit to all questions?
Clown: As fit as ten groats for the hand of an attorney, as your French crown for your taffeta punk, as Tib's rush for Tom's forefinger, as a pancake for Shrove-Tuesday, a morris for May-day, as the nail to his hole, a cuckold to his horn, as a scolding quean to a wrangling knave, as a nun's lip to the friar's mouth; nay, as the pudding to the skin.

Mrs Ternan as the Countess Rousillon and Mr Lewis Ball as the Clown in *All's Well that Ends Well* (*Mary Evans Picture Library*)

Lear. I tax not you, you elements, with unkindness;
I never gave you kingdom, call'd you children,
You owe me no subscription.   *Act III. Scene II.*

We must remember when we look at Lavache's more obscene similes (for an example read the start of Act V, scene 2) that the Elizabethans did not find humour concerning bodily functions, such as breaking wind, the vulgarity it is today. Such things were acceptable subjects for humour and were laughed at by people of all classes. Playful bawdiness was as much enjoyed by the court as by the commoner. The humour often took the form of puns, as in the following exchange between the clown and a musician in *Othello*:

Clown: Are these, I pray you, wind instruments?
First musician: Ay, marry, are they, sir.
Clown: O, thereby hangs a tail.
First musician: Whereby hangs a tale, sir?
Clown: Marry, sir, by many a wind-instrument that I know.

Fools are most often found in Shakespeare's comedies, but they also figure in the tragedies, and the most sublimely wise fool is to be found in *King Lear*. Despite his knowledge of the King's folly, the clown follows the mad Lear with the utmost loyalty, even when common sense tells him it is not the wisest thing to do. Like Feste and Touchstone, he is a domestic jester with the usual licence of free speech.

Lear's fool displays one of the traditional tricks of the Elizabethan stage clown: he hands his cockscomb and bauble to anyone he thinks more foolish than himself—in this case to Kent and Lear. The same practice is referred to by Lavache in his comic discussion with Lafeu on the difference between a knave and a fool: 'And I would give his wife my bauble, sir, to do her service.'

It was thought in the past that Lear's fool was an idiot. The writer Francis Douce calls him a 'mere natural with a considerable share of cunning'. But he has a very real knowledge of the folly of those around him: he taunts Goneril, gives shrewd advice to the doomed King and is aware that it is Lear, not himself, who is the fool. Absurdity is inherent in the tragedy. It is plainly ridiculous for Lear to relinquish his kingdom and expect still to be accorded the respect due to a monarch; his unreal demands on his children are fated to bring disillusionment. Without the fool, Lear's tragedy of foolish misjudgement would itself teeter on the brink of absurdity. The fool's observations on Lear's tyrannical outbursts act as a kind of chorus, pointing out the absurdity of the King's actions to the audience.

Lear: When were you wont to be so full of songs, sirrah?
Fool: I have us'd it, nuncle, e'er since thou madst thy daughters thy mothers; for when thou gavst them the rod, and put'st down thine own breeches . . .

Although the fool enjoys the same freedom of speech as any court jester of the time, he must recognize his position as an inferior and disguise his trenchant comments with a bit of nonsense—as in his taunt of Goneril: 'May not an ass know when the cart draws the horse? Whoops, Jug! I love thee.'

When the fool heroically follows Lear to the wild, stormy heath it is Edgar disguised as poor, mad Tom, who assumes the role of counterpart to the King's madness, while the fool's comments become more serious:

Lear: Is it the fashion that discarded fathers
Should have thus little mercy on their flesh?
Judicious punishment! 'twas this flesh begot
Those pelican daughters.
Edgar: Pillicock sat on Pillicock Hill.
Alow, alow, loo, loo!
Fool: This cold night will turn us all to fools and madmen.

Although Shakespeare's clowns belong to certain recognizable types—such as rough country bumpkins and intellectual wits—they all perform a function unique in the history of drama. As the scholar R. H. Goldsmith points out: 'Shakespeare had come to realise . . . that the comic spirit breathes most freely in the person of a somewhat detached observer.'

7 On Stage

As we have seen, in Elizabethan times the clown was as important as the serious actor in attracting audiences to Shakespeare's plays. The two favourite comedians, William Kempe and Robert Armin, were the first stage clowns of any note. Shakespeare delighted in the wit of the jester, particularly as interpreted by Armin, and much of the comic 'business' in his plays may be drawn from Armin's improvisations.

Kempe, as well as being a clown and a shareholder of the Globe Theatre, was a composer of jigs. When he was well established in his career—one which had brought him renown on the Continent, as well as in England—the clown, with delightful eccentricity, danced a morris all the way from London to Norwich.

'Comparisons are odorous', observes Dogberry in *Much Ado About Nothing*, but it is safe to say that German theatre of this period was less entertaining than its English counterpart, consisting mainly of serious, moralizing drama. The arrival of troupes of English travelling players in Germany brought a welcome

The Cirque Napoléon in the nineteenth century. Later to be named the Cirque d'Hiver, the building was opened by Napoleon III in 1852 and was one of the many permanent buildings constructed in Paris at the time to house the increasingly successful circuses (*BBC Hulton Picture Library*)

note of levity to the scene, and the most important member of the comic dramas for which these theatrical troupes were famous was the clown.

The actors quickly learned Low German for their performances and were reinforced by German actors. The English clowns were masters of gesture and facial expression and their acts featured superb fooling, expert dancing, fencing and acrobatics. Even when Germans played the comic roles, the clowns were still known as 'English Fool' or 'English John'.

Each clown had an individual style, the most popular of which was that of Pickelherring, a clown invented by the English actor Robert Reynolds. Reynolds arrived in Germany by 1616 as a member of Robert Browne and John Green's company—of which he later became the manager.

Pickelherring won an enviable reputation during a career that lasted for more than twenty years. He sported a costume of a vaguely military style, several sizes too large for him. He wore a sword by his side and a huge Tyrolean hat on his head, in addition to a ruff round his neck. He was skilled in miming, laughter, terror and drunkenness and had the audience giggling before he spoke a word.

Among the various roles played by Pickelherring were a silly servant, a bearer of urgent letters (which, of course, never arrived at their destination) and a hangman. Pickelherring also raised laughs by parodying the other actors and comically asking his audience for their views on the action.

Robert Browne and Thomas Green led their troupes in Germany for a long time, from about 1590 until 1626. A rather disparaging contemporary description of them comes from Fynes Moryson, a scholar and Secretary to the Lord Deputy of Ireland who visited Frankfurt in 1592:

Germany hath some few wandering comedians more deserving pity than praise, for the serious parts are dully penned, and worse acted, and the mirth they make is ridiculous . . . So as I remember that when some of our cast despised stage players came out of England into Germany, and played at Frankfort at the time of the Mart, having neither a complete number of actors, nor any good apparel, nor any ornament of the stage, yet the Germans, not understanding a word they said, both men and women, flocked wonderfully to see their gesture and action rather than hear them, speaking English which they understood not, and pronouncing pieces and patches of English plays, which myself and some English men there present could not hear without great wearisomeness.

Other stage clowns emerged from the increasing creative freedom of the professional actor. In France, for example, there appeared the character of Badin, a simpleton, not altogether a fool and not distinguished by a special costume. Bobo is a similar figure in Spain, a comic servant type influenced by the Italian comedians' Harlequin. Later, in the 1800s, came the development of the love-lorn, pathetic Pierrot by Jean-Gaspard Deburau, who dominated Paris's Théâtre des Funambules.

The Funambules opened in 1816 as a booth for acrobats, rope dancers, dog acts and *revues-féeries*, or pantomimes, with the old Italian stories featuring Harlequin. The theatre became a permanent playhouse, marvellously equipped, including apparatus for a real waterfall. Like most Paris theatres it had never received a government licence to perform spoken plays; these were regarded as potentially subversive. So, basing its action on the pantomime plots, the Funambules presented wonderful feats of tight-rope walking, tumbling, quick-change, flying traps and slapstick, accompanied by dancing and popular music.

Grimaldi as Clown, from a contemporary portrait published in 1818 (*BBC Hulton Picture Library*)

Twenty years before the Funambules opened, Deburau had been born in Bohemia—then under Austrian rule, now part of Czechoslovakia. He was the youngest member of a family of touring acrobats and spent a rootless childhood in a Europe battered by the Napoleonic wars. Deburau's mother died young and he grew into a tall, dreamy, taciturn fellow—a clumsy acrobat ridiculed by his more agile brothers and sisters.

The family settled in Paris in 1814, and eight years later Deburau began to appear with his father at the Funambules as a buffoon with a talent for elegant and savage mimicry. In 1826, when he was thirty years old, his father died, leaving him free to sign his own contract with the theatre to play Pierrot, the white-faced clown.

Pierrot was one of the characters in the harlequinade, a type of play featuring the ever-popular Harlequin, brought to France by the Italian commedia dell' arte. The tale was a simple one of virtuous young love between Harlequin and Columbine, thwarted by parents and rivals, Pantaloon and Pierrot, Scaramouch and Clown. The rival was comically and heartlessly pursued, assaulted and betrayed throughout the pantomime until the final scene of reconciliation.

Before Deburau's time, the Pierrot was a loosely-defined clown figure in the Italian comedy—a figure of fun identified with Gros-Guillaume, the French fool who played in front of Cardinal Richelieu with a face covered with baker's flour.

By the eighteenth century, the white-faced clown had established himself in supporting roles in many of the harlequinades in France, although the commedia dell'arte itself was barred from Paris during the last years of the reign of Louis XIV.

111

Pierrot was a buffoon and trickster, the ever-successful rival of Harlequin for the love of Columbine. He was known variously as Pierrot, Paillasse ('Old Strawbags'), Pedrolino, Gilles or Pierre.

Deburau's performances of Pierrot gained a cult following among the French. In his skilful hands the character changed from one of country-bumpkin innocence to one endowed with a measure of cunning. Yet at the same time his Pierrot could convey the pathos of the human condition. The lively and tough audience who sat in the 'gods' of the theatre in this revolutionary quarter of Paris loved him. He dominated them despite his enforced silence—for Deburau was a wholly silent mime. In the dimly-lit, stuffy little Funambules Theatre, he utterly captivated his audience. In a few moments he could move them from laughter to tears and back again.

Without words, he depended on startling visual methods of communication. These included *cascades*, or balletic fights, *sauts*, startling and often dangerous leaps up and down counter-weighted trap-doors and *trucs*, bizarre, instant changes of scenery or props so that a cooling ice cream, say, might be transformed into a flickering Roman candle in Pierrot's hand.

As Pierrot, Deburau came into his own. He dominated the harlequinade and instilled Pierrot with his own mocking, slyly malicious, charming but bitter personality. He discarded the ruff of the commedia clown and donned the black skullcap which became an indispensable part of the French Pierrot's costume.

One day in 1836 while out walking with his wife, Deburau killed a seventeen-year-old youth because the boy had dared to mock him. He was acquitted, but the real-life tragedy inspired in his Pierrot an altogether darker quality. He became a stark, sad and fearful figure. The later 1840s saw the development of the pantomime of death. *Le Marchand d'habits*, in which Pierrot kills an old clothes merchant so that he is able to attend a society ball, became Deburau's signature sketch. One hundred years later it was superbly and movingly re-created by the French actor and director, Jean Louis Barrault in the famous film celebration of the Funambules, *Les Enfants du Paradis*.

Pierrot died with his creator in 1846, but he was destined to live again as the masterful white clown of modern times.

In Britain the theatre fell on hard times during the mid-1600s, when the Puritan regime of Oliver Cromwell banned the performance of plays in public. Puritan opposition to the theatre had been growing steadily since the beginning of the seventeenth century and in 1642 the Puritan-dominated Parliament passed a law making participation in theatrical performance in public a penal offence. This effectively stole a livelihood from actors of the time—apart, that is, from those who defied the ban and performed in 'drolls'.

Drolls were short comic scenes based on Shakespeare and on biblical themes which were performed under the Commonwealth at country fairs and in the smaller theatres—in between raids by Cromwell's soldiers. The drolls were often rather indecent. A contemporary illustration shows the actor Robert Cox in the role of a simpleton carrying a somewhat suggestive long French loaf.

The Puritans were not against drama as such, for under the Commonwealth plays continued to be performed in schools and private houses. However, public performances were thought to provide audiences with the opportunity for subversive political activities. Also, dramatists had espoused the Royalist cause, and so were regarded with suspicion by the Puritans. Other objections were based on social and sometimes religious grounds; the hard work and self-

The invention of the circus is attributed to a one-time English soldier called Philip Astley. His amphitheatre was opened in 1770 and was the home of the first modern circus clown; this is how the amphitheatre appeared in 1812 (*Mary Evans Picture Library*)

Andrew Ducrow, a skilled horseman and circus performer, built up the English circus in the first half of the nineteenth century. His clowns were in great demand all over the Continent (*Mary Evans Picture Library*)

above: The Spanish clown Charlie
Rivels as Diva at Munich's Circus-
Krone in 1971. Charlie, who is in
his eighties, still clowns for a
living (*ZEFA: photo by Kurt
Scholz*)

opposite right: Early circus clowns
were much involved in riding acts.
This clown to the bareback rider
appears on the cover of 'The
Million' (*Mansell Collection*)

REGISTERED AT THE
G. P. O. AS
A NEWSPAPER.

THE MILLION

· EDITED ·
= BY =
GEO. NEWNES.

No. 39, Vol. 2.]   FOR THE WEEK ENDING SATURDAY, DECEMBER 17, 1892.   [Price One Penny.

"HOUP-LA!"

discipline were expected of a loyal British public did not accord well with such allegedly frivolous pastimes as going to the theatre.

In 1656, two years before the death of Cromwell, the playwright William Davenant was allowed to produce in public *The Siege of Rhodes*, an entertainment with music. Actors and playwrights were further encouraged when Charles II and his court returned from exile in 1660; derelict theatres sprang into life once more and England embarked on a glorious age for the performing arts. For the aristocracy and educated classes there was the elegant, subtle wit of Restoration drama; Dryden, Congreve, Wycherley and Etherege stylishly satirized the greed, hypocrisy and philistinism they saw around them.

Alongside such sophisticated offerings there grew up a form of theatre peculiar to England which appealed to a wider audience. This was pantomime. English pantomime (which, with its noisy exuberance, has little in common with wordless pantomime) evolved from the dregs of the commedia dell'arte, which in Italy, was now in a state of decline. The once-brilliant scenarios had become hackneyed; the actors lacked spirit; the satire had lost its bite. But some of the characters of the Italian comedy developed new lives of their own. Just as Pierrot would later be transformed by Jean-Gaspard Deburau, so Harlequin entered a new phase of existence on the English stage, interpreted there by a dancing master named John Weaver. Weaver, also the manager of Covent Garden Theatre, had seen Harlequin performed at Paris fairs and by Italian players in England.

Weaver's early pantomimes—then called harlequinades—owed part of their success to the elaborate stage machinery with which seventeenth-century theatres were equipped and which made possible all sorts of comic transformations. From its very beginnings pantomime was the theatre of transformation, of magic brought about by a wave of Harlequin's magic wand.

In the early 1700s Weaver's success was consolidated by a brilliant mime, John Rich, who catered to the ever-increasing vogue for pantomime at Lincoln's Inn Fields Theatre, which he had inherited from his father. Rich, who worked under the stage name of Lun, turned Harlequin into an irrepressible prankster whose personality was to be echoed later in the century by the rascally Clown. Through the brilliant imagination of Joseph Grimaldi this worldly-wise rapscallion stole the show from Harlequin and eventually became the hero of the piece.

'Joey', as Grimaldi was universally known, was the illegitimate son of an elderly ballet master who had spent the first forty years of his life in theatres in Italy and France. His mother was a young Cockney dancing girl. Joey's first performance took place at the age of two years and four months at the Sadler's Wells Theatre on Easter Monday, 1781.

Grimaldi's memoirs, rewritten by Charles Dickens, show the clown to have been an enchanting man, naive and unworldly, yet at the same time highly imaginative. Richard Findlater, author of *King of Clowns*, a biography of Grimaldi, points out the many inaccuracies and omissions in Dickens' portrait, but as it stands, we are provided with an object lesson in humanity and uprightness in a world where drunkenness and greed were common.

Grimaldi's father was an eccentric man, whose whims may have provided the inspiration for the son's comic inventions. One story from the memoirs describes how the elder Grimaldi bought a piece of land in Lambeth in the depths of winter. He and his son decorated the trees there with an immense

opposite above: The internationally acclaimed Russian clown, Oleg Popov, in a sketch at the Moscow State Circus. Like many Russian and East European clowns, Popov wears little make-up: things grotesque or freakish are not part of the modern Russian clown's repertoire. Popov is shown (*opposite below*) in a sketch with an eastern theme (*Vision International: photos by Paolo Koch*)

quantity of artificial flowers and fruit to give an idea of the garden's summer glory.

However, Grimaldi's father was not only eccentric; he was harsh and cruel. Grimaldi may not have suffered the sheer wretchedness that other poor children of his time did, but he was certainly overworked and punished with uncommon cruelty by his aged father. One method the old man used to discipline his son was to put him in a cage which was hoisted up to the flies. When the young Grimaldi practised his pantomime off the stage for the amusement of the company, his father thrashed him.

The ballet master's demands on his son certainly seem more than a little abnormal if a story in Dickens' book is to be believed. On one occasion Grimaldi senior feigned death in order to find out the true feelings towards him of Joey and his brother John. Joey saw through the ruse and fell into the fits of weeping he knew were expected of him. His brother, not so worldly-wise, skipped with joy at what he saw as a happy release from parental tyranny. At this, their father arose in paroxysms of rage and beat the hapless John within an inch of his life, while Joey prudently ran off to hide. He was discovered four hours later and

above: A cartoon of Grimaldi as a drunkard (*BBC Hulton Picture Library*) and (*right*) Grimaldi as a clown and thief in the company of Harlequin, Columbine and Pantaloon, by George Cruikshank, whose drawings appear in Grimaldi's memoirs (*Mary Evans Picture Library*)

opposite right: A programme for Covent Garden Grand Circus (*BBC Hulton Picture Library*)

right: Grimaldi in *Harlequin and Padmanaba,* 1811 (*Fotomas*)

was reunited with his father, who welcomed him with open arms, satisfied, for the moment at least, that he had the love of one of his sons.

Besides being a teacher of ballet, the old Grimaldi was a dancer and actor in English pantomime, in which he played the parts of Pantaloon and Clown. According to Richard Findlater's research, he was not a very good clown; he played 'a low-comedy fool, with an obscenity too much for English taste, and an inability to make himself understood'.

Young Joey's growing fame as a comic dancer can be attributed to the influence of his mother, once a member of the *corps de ballet* at Drury Lane, who was famous in a small way for her character dancing. She it was who taught Joey the basic techniques of dancing.

In his boyhood, Joey played dwarfs, old hags and animal parts on the stage, often in company with his father as Clown. A story in the memoirs tells of how Joey was taking the role of a monkey in his first season at Sadler's Wells. He was attached by a chain to the waist of Clown, and in one scene he was swung rapidly round and round on the end of it. One particular night, when this turn was in progress, the chain broke and the tiny Joey was flung miraculously into the arms of an old fellow watching the performance.

Dickens' book shows that, glamorous as the life of a Regency actor might be, Grimaldi was extremely hard-working and was prematurely aged by the exertions of his calling. In his early years he played at both Sadler's Wells and Drury Lane Theatres on the same day and would have to run like a hare between the two in order to appear on time. According to one story—doubtless apocryphal—he once covered the distance, about two miles, in eight minutes.

Old Grimaldi died in 1788 when Joey was ten years old. John took the opportunity of running off to sea, eschewing the theatrical career intended for him by his father. Joey stayed in the theatre and came under the influence of Jean Baptist Dubois, the French tumbler and dancer, who, until he joined Drury Lane Theatre in 1789, had been a circus performer.

Dubois was the first to introduce colour into the white costume of the Pierrot. One of his most popular feats was the traditional egg hornpipe. This dance

opposite right: The thirty-first annual service attended by clowns in honour of Grimaldi at Holy Trinity church, Dalston, East London (*Keystone Press Agency*)

120

involved a dozen or so eggs, which were placed at certain points marked upon the stage. The orchestra would strike up the strains of a hornpipe, and Dubois, blindfolded and wearing wooden clogs, would perform his dance across the stage without breaking a single egg.

Grimaldi was also strongly influenced by Charles Dibdin and his brother Tom. Both men were the authors of hundreds of songs and Tom was a director of Sadler's Wells. It was Tom who, in 1800, decided to try the innovation of having two clowns in the pantomime instead of the usual one. Dubois played Gobble the Eating Clown, while Joey, who shared top billing with him, was Guzzle, the Drinking Clown. Both were a huge success.

From that time, however, Dubois was gradually eclipsed by Grimaldi, who was becoming noted for his powerful miming and his skill with the broadsword in dramatic fights 'to the death'. Comic duelling was Grimaldi's forte; in one stage duel at the Wells he and his opponent shot the seconds and shook hands over their corpses.

Like Dubois, who left Sadler's Wells at the end of 1801, Joey had been experimenting with his clown's dress and face. And in 1806 the clown was given a vehicle in which to display both his new character and his fine comic powers. At Christmas that year Covent Garden Theatre produced its most successful harlequinade, *Harlequin and Mother Goose*, or *The Golden Egg*. It was immensely popular with the public and ran for ninety-two performances. The main reason for its popularity was the genius of Grimaldi.

His clown's face was covered with geometrical patches of paint; his clothes were adorned with frills, spots and bands of colour in mocking imitation of the dandy of the time. He was a glutton who would swallow strings of sausages and platefuls of tarts—props he has passed on to the modern circus clown; he sang nonsense songs; he performed physical tricks, took pratfalls and administered slapstick thrashings. His infectious, raucous laugh was echoed by delighted spectators.

Many of the jokes Grimaldi invented were entirely original and depended mainly on constructing things out of unlikely objects. He would turn himself into a hussar by donning coal-scuttle 'boots', candlestick 'spurs' and red pantaloons. A post-chaise was made out of a basket and cheeses. Grimaldi would enter first as the local squire, Sir Feeble Sordid or Lord Humpty Dandy, and then reveal himself as Clown.

Grimaldi has been called the Michelangelo of buffoonery. He was particularly famed for his comic songs. With his writers and arrangers, the Dibdin brothers and Charles Farley, he infused them with biting social satire. The songs were on everybody's lips in much the same way as were those of the Beatles in the 1960s. 'Hot Codlins', one of Joe Grimaldi's most popular comic songs, was still being sung on the stage thirty years after his death. Hot codlins were roasted apples sold in the streets of London at the time. The song is not particularly funny when read, but as interpreted by Grimaldi, with humorous reflections and grimaces, it was a perennial favourite.

A little old woman her living got
By selling codlins, hot, hot, hot;
And this little woman, who codlins sold,
Tho' her codlins were hot, she felt herself cold.
So to keep herself warm, she thought it no sin
To fetch for herself a quartern of gin.

The last word would be roared by the audience—at which Grimaldi would respond, 'Oh, for shame!' The song continued in the same manner with the audience roaring the last word of each stanza and joining Grimaldi in a nonsense chorus.

> This little old woman set off in a trot,
> To fetch her quartern of hot, hot, hot!
> She swallowed one glass, and it was so nice,
> She tipped off another in a trice;
> The glass she filled till the bottle shrunk,
> And this little woman they say got (drunk).
>
> This little old woman, while muzzy she got,
> Some boys stole her codlins, hot, hot, hot.
> Powder under her pan put, and in it round stones:
> Says the little old woman: 'These apples have bones!'
> The powder the pan in her face did send,
> Which sent the old woman on her latter (end).
>
> The little old woman then up she got,
> All in a fury, hot, hot, hot.
> Says she, 'Such boys, sure, never were known;
> They never will let an old woman alone.
> Now here is a moral, round let it buz—
> If you mean to sell codlins, never get (muz).

The essence of Grimaldi's performances lay in his dynamic energy. When his strength began to fail him, men would wait in the wings to massage his legs as soon as he came off stage. Throughout his career he suffered broken bones, wrenched muscles and other injuries brought on by numberless comic kicks and beatings. Grimaldi bore such mishaps with professional poise; once when an unloaded pistol triggered off when he was pulling it from his boot in a mock fight, thus setting fire to his stocking, he played on to the end of the performance. Afterwards, he was discovered to be quite seriously burned and was encouraged to rest. For a short time he recovered at his new home, surrounded by the plump breeding pigeons which had been his solace since the untimely death in childbirth of his young wife. On another occasion, when performing Clown in the provinces, Grimaldi was supposed to shoot up through a trapdoor in the stage; but the ropes holding him snapped and he fell back, hurting himself badly on the hard cellar floor. Again, however, he insisted on completing his performance.

Such accidents were common on the pantomime stage. Grimaldi's insistence on playing at two theatres a night—on one occasion, three—certainly contributed to his early disablement. He once claimed that during the course of his stage career every bone in his body had been broken or injured. Spasms and cramps continued to assail him until he could no longer stand. Broken-hearted, he gave his farewell performance to the public at Drury Lane Theatre seated on a chair at the footlights.

Grimaldi's success can be summed up in that elusive concept 'style'. To the eighteenth-century man or woman style was all-important; it did not matter what you did so much as *how* you did it. Grimaldi inherited a centuries-old

clowning tradition and added to it his own unique style, transforming what now seems unpromising written material to create a new, distinctively English type of clown. His was a clown which, for the first time, did not rely simply on the slow wit of the rustic yokel outsmarted by a shrewder partner; he was a smart urban satirist, poking fun at the vices of the age, getting his laughs out of transforming everyday objects and gilding every situation with his inimitable and immortal comic gift.

In his crippled middle age, Grimaldi taught his son, young Joe, the rudiments of clowning, and the boy succeeded his father in the part he had created. Young Joe, who was the son of Grimaldi and his second wife, Mary Bristow, seemed destined for a success almost as great as his father's. But sadly, he led a life of drunken debauchery and died after a mental breakdown when he was little more than thirty years old. Typically, Grimaldi refused to be ungenerous to a son whom others saw as an ungrateful wastrel. He attributed the boy's bad conduct to a blow on the head from a policeman's truncheon during a drunken brawl outside an inn.

Deeply grieved by the death of his son, and later that of his second wife, after a long paralysing illness, Grimaldi lived on alone, his family and his days of fame and laughter things of the past. But he found company and cheer among old friends near his home in Southampton Street, Pentonville Hill, whom he visited nightly, carried to and from on the back of the landlord of the local inn, William Cook. On the evening of 31 May 1837, Grimaldi said goodnight to Cook, as usual: 'God bless you, my boy, I shall be ready for you tomorrow night!' Grimaldi died that night in his sleep, aged fifty-eight, and was buried at St James's Chapel close by.

The British public had taken Joe Grimaldi to their hearts and exploded with laughter at his entertainment, a spectacle which had come a long way from the simpler, more innocent humour enjoyed in country parishes. Cheered and carried through the streets whenever he was recognized, Grimaldi was—and has remained—the 'king of clowns'. In his honour circus people still call a clown a 'Joey', and 'Grimaldi acts' are still part of the modern clown repertoire.

In the past, clowns from all over the world held a simple memorial service every year for Grimaldi in the church where he lies buried. More recently the service has been held in Holy Trinity Church, Dalston, East London, where, in February 1978, clowns assembled to celebrate the 200th anniversary of the birth of this inspired comic genius.

During the last years of his life Grimaldi penned or dictated his memoirs. He concluded them with this bit of verse:

> Life is a game we are bound to play—
> The wise enjoy it, fools grow sick of it;
> Losers, we find, have the stakes to pay,
> The winners may laugh, for that's the trick of it.

opposite left: Grimaldi's style of clowning lives on in the props of this Victorian Christmas pantomime clown. A drawing by J. A. Fitzgerald, 1877 (*Mansell Collection*)

8 Charivari in the Circus

The creation of the circus in the late eighteenth century added a new dimension to clowning. While continuing to dance, sing and act as he had on the stage, the clown acquired talents which were better suited to a large arena, in which many people were too far away to appreciate the traditional comic routines. The circus clown skilfully burlesqued horse-riding, juggling and wire-walking. He became a spectacular acrobat and tumbler and—particularly in France—a musician. Because of the increased need for visual acting, the clown developed into a superlative mime.

Thanks to the great enterprise of travelling showmen and circus proprietors in both Europe and America, the clowns reached audiences in far-flung areas, delighting frontiersmen of the Great Plains, Welsh coal miners and Russian peasants, as well as city-dwellers. Many of the travelling circuses were French. The oldest of these was founded by Jacques Tourniaire shortly after the French Revolution. It was another French circus—the Cirque Napoléon Rancy—which gave the Egyptians their first glimpse of circus clowning at the opening of the Suez Canal in 1868.

The sawdust ring seems to have been a British invention. Before anyone heard of the great circus families—the Baileys, Chipperfields, Cookes, Fossets, Knies, Krones, Ringlings, and Sangers—a celebrated but poor soldier bought a field near Westminster Bridge called Halfpenny Hatch. Here he gave exhibitions of vaulting on two or three horses and sabre fighting such as was practised by the hussars.

The man was Philip Astley and the year 1768. Astley had been born twenty-six years earlier in the little English village of Newcastle-under-Lyme. His father was a cabinet-maker who wanted his son to follow the same worthy trade. But from a very young age, Astley had an abiding love for horses. By the time he had reached seventeen, he had run away to join the Fifth Regiment of Dragoons, for whom he worked as a rough rider and horse-breaker.

Astley became a non-commissioned officer and won military glory by capturing the French standard in the Battle of Emsdorf in Hesse in 1760. When he left his regiment six years later, among his few assets was a white horse called Gibraltar, which had been given to him by his colonel. With Gibraltar and two more horses purchased later, he gave performances of his marvellous riding skill and sword play at Halfpenny Hatch. The arena was formed in a circle surrounded by a wooden fence. Astley had discovered that if he rode fast in a circle he could stand up on the horse's back—held in place by centrifugal force. And so he traced the first circus ring. In the middle, on a platform, stood Astley's bride with a drum and two fifers, who called attention to the show. The hat was passed round after the performance.

The venture was successful enough for Astley to buy more land nearby a year or two later. Here he built a permanent circus, a wooden building with a circular

opposite left: 'The Entry of the Clowns', painted by Jules Garnier in 1890 (*Mary Evans Picture Library*)

arena open to the sky, overlooked by stands and enclosed by railings. There were galleries for the gentry. Stables were attached to the main building. Astley called it his 'New British Riding School'. This predecessor of the modern circus was first opened to the public in 1770. A commemorative plaque marks its site on London's South Bank where the extension to St Thomas's Hospital now stands.

However, not all circus historians accept Astley's riding exhibition as the first circus. The writer George Speaight, for example, feels that such a claim is an over-simplification; he asserts that performances in a circular or squared enclosure, with acrobats, rope-dancers and trained animals, had been taking place here and there in Europe for more than one hundred years before Astley established his famous amphitheatre. They took place in bear gardens and in theatres shaped like bear gardens in London, in the Fechthaus in Nuremburg and in the Hetz Amphitheatre in Vienna. Speaight adds that what Astley *does* deserve credit for is the drive and business skill he employed to popularize the idea of the circus throughout England and France.

If equestrian displays were not an innovation of Astley's, the introduction of a clown into the same arena probably was. Astley's comic, dubbed Mr Merryman, indulged in the now time-honoured practice of cracking jokes with the ringmaster. Mr Merryman was ornately dressed in a close-fitting jacket with a frilled collar, striped hose and a wig, from which sprouted three peacock feathers. He appears in Dickens' *Master Humphrey's Clock*, in a reference to 'the clown who ventured such familiarities with the military man in boots'.

One of the more interesting clowns who worked for Astley was a man named Dicky Usher, who joined the circus from the Royal Amphitheatre, Liverpool. He was probably the first and only comic to use jokes written for him by the scholars of Westminster School, who vied with one another to see which of their gags won the best response from the audience.

The best jokes became part of Usher's repertoire, which, needless to say, contained rich comic inventions of his own. It was Usher's job to open each

performance of the circus, which followed a play presented on a stage which formed part of the amphitheatre. Some of its audience stood in the ring, and were called 'half-pricers'. When the play ended, they left; fresh sawdust was strewn and Usher would leap into the ring with his famous entrance line, 'Here we are again!'

Usher amused Londoners on one occasion by travelling on the River Thames in a bathtub drawn by four geese, Gibble, Gabble, Garble and Gobble. He covered the distance from Westminster to Waterloo Bridge, where he disembarked and entered a carriage pulled by eight fat cats which, if the story is to be believed, transported him to the theatre, about half a mile away. Other clowns tried the same eccentric journey with the geese and tub, without success, until someone gave the game away and spoiled the joke. The tub was pulled, not by geese, but by a boat sailing out of sight a little farther down the river.

Fire was always a great hazard at the circus. When, in 1841, Astley's had been gutted by fire for the third time, Dicky Usher and William Batty, a rider, drew up plans for a new amphitheatre to replace it. When completed in 1842 it became known as the Royal Amphitheatre of Arts, enjoying the patronage of members of the royal family. By this time the circus was run by Andrew Ducrow, then one of the most renowned circus performers in the world. He was skilled in rope-dancing, mime and animal training as well as in management. He originated the *poses plastiques*, in which the rider represented a series of classical statues on the back of a horse cantering round the ring at twenty miles an hour.

For twenty years, until his death in 1842, Ducrow built up Astley's circus to a high level of professionalism and made English clowns much in demand all over

'The little tight-rope walker', drawn by the Flemish artist Pannemaker, in c. 1815 (*Mary Evans Picture Library*)

following pages: 'Im Circus' by Otto Walter (*Mansell Collection*)

129

'The Royal Circus' by Thomas
Rowlandson (1756-1827) and
Augustus Welby Northmore Pugin
(1812-52). As a young man Pugin
had designed scenery and theatrical
machinery for the Dury Lane
Theatre (*Mansell Collection*)

opposite right: Keaton's stony
expression dominates a poster
advertising *The General* to the
Russian public (*Finler*)

the Continent. Artists who had performed with him later set up their own
circuses. Among them was Pablo Fanques, in reality an English mulatto named
William Darby who indulged himself in the circus fashion for assuming exotic-
sounding names.

At one point in his career Ducrow went to Paris to appear in and share the
profits of a circus owned by Astley and run by the Venetian-born Franconi
family.

One of the English clowns who performed in Paris was William Wallett, who
called himself a Shakespearian jester. Looking back, it is rather difficult to
understand the appeal of this self-important man. Wallett's act involved strutting
round the ring and assuming studied poses while uttering Shakespearian jests.
He wore a costume of tights, hessian boots, tasselled cap and brocaded tunic. He
made no effort to win the emotional sympathy of the audience; nor did he offer
such diversions as tumbling or acrobatics.

Wallett had come to Astley's after working with Pablo Fanques' circus, where,
on a crowded benefit night, the gallery collapsed, killing Fanques' wife and
injuring Wallett's. The clown worked for a brief time in the near-bankrupt
Ryan's circus before he joined Astley's. After a visit to Windsor Castle to present
Queen Victoria with four lion cubs, Wallett took to calling himself 'the Queen's
jester'. His attempts at self-aggrandizement were so outrageous that he managed

previous pages: An advertising poster for Buster Keaton's film *The General*, a comic masterpiece of the silent era (*Finler*)

Members of the Ballet Rambert in *Pierrot Lunaire* (*photo by Reg Wilson*)

A Czech mime company at the Théatre of the Balustrade (*photo by Reg Wilson*)

to quarrel with Dicky Usher's successor, Tom Barry, who left Astley's in a huff in 1853 to keep a public house near the theatre.

Barry was a rather more human figure than Wallett and by all accounts a much funnier one. He was a riding comic and would begin his act sitting on a tiny donkey. Dressed in a close-fitting costume and white nightcap embellished with two feathers, he often played a drunken Irishman or farrier. His favourite character was that of Mr William Button of Tooley Street in 'The Tailor's Journey to Brentford'. This entertainment, called a 'hippo-comedietta', was a traditional skit on horseback which involved a military tailor—always considered the worst rider in any regiment.

A variation of 'The Tailor's Journey' was the 'Peter Jenkins Act', which, in a similar form, is still seen in some circuses today. The ringmaster is told that the bareback rider has had an accident and is not able to appear. The ringmaster apologizes to the audience, whereupon a seemingly drunk and decrepit fellow rises from the audience and elbows his way into the ring to complain. He is invited to ride the horse himself. To loud encouraging cheers from the audience, he clambers awkwardly on to the back of the horse—no doubt a spirited one— and reveals himself as a skilful acrobat in tights and spangles.

By the middle of the nineteenth century Paris had become the liveliest centre for circus and clowning. One colourful showman, Louis Dejean, was the most successful circus proprietor of the time. Three of the circuses in Paris were born of his enterprise. One of them—the Cirque Napoléon, opened by Napoleon III in 1852—still exists under the name of the Cirque d'Hiver. It was originally presented in a small ring which permitted a more intimate kind of clowning than was possible in the larger arenas.

An Astley's clown, possibly Tom Barry, convinces Thames-side onlookers that he is drawn upstream by four geese (*Mary Evans Picture Library*)

137

In Paris, tumblers, musicians, clowns, tight-rope walkers, horse riders and numerous other talented artists from all over the world found scope for innovation. The English clowns John and William Price were a great attraction in Paris, where they were engaged throughout the winter. (The two men later established the Circo Price in Madrid.) They played violin and flute duets while balancing on the tops of unsupported ladders or while performing acts of tumbling or contortion. Like Tom Barry, they wore tight-fitting costumes to emphasize their athletic bodies. Their faces were plastered with white make-up and they wore grotesque three-pointed wigs. Their musical tricks and their costumes influenced French clowns, notably the memorable Auriol, whose amazing feats of balancing earned him the nickname 'L'Homme Oiseau' ('The Bird-man').

Auriol played a French horn while standing on his head on a bottle. His last appearance was in 1873.

Burlesque music began to play a large part in the entrées of French clowns. The Pinauds, for instance, had an act in which one of the clowns would try to play a guitar, only to be interrupted by a musical cannon fired at his back. This troupe also performed pantomimes. In one of these a bull attacks a peasant, who drives off the beast with an umbrella. He is about to triumph in this daring feat when his partner decides to set fire to his hat. The hat explodes and in mock anguish the clown lifts his hands to the skies. A shower of hats and caps of all shapes and sizes pour down upon him. He tries them on but not one will fit. He ends the act by again lifting up his hands in despair.

The 'wrong hat' is a bit of comic business often employed in various forms by clowns today. A fire can only be extinguished by a clown wearing a fireman's hat; and a lot of time is wasted, hilariously, as the clown turns up again and again in anything but the right hat.

English clowns were particularly noted for their tumbling and acrobatic prowess. Lavater Lee, one of the Hanlon-Lee troupe of clowns, was said to have been able to leap over forty horses. Twenty-five years after their London debut in 1847, the clowns appeared in Paris, where they won the acclaim of French audiences, including the novelist Émile Zola, who described their 'burlesque duels, tipsy misadventures, crazy juggling with household furniture, upsets in stage coaches and collisions of railway trains'.

The need for visual effects did not altogether exclude the talking clown. One well-loved talking clown on the Continent was Billy Hayden, a black minstrel who performed in white face. He would come into the ring on a donkey and begin his act by saying: 'I, too, was once a pretty young lady. A witch came by with an ugly little boy. She took me, the pretty little girl, out of the perambulator, and she put in my place the ugly little boy. And ever since then I've been an ugly little boy.' Hayden was often accompanied by a trained pig.

One of the most enduring clown characters from the late nineteenth century is the auguste. There are several theories of how the auguste first came into being. The writer Willson Disher claims that the first to play the part in France was a clown called James Guyon, whose costume consisted of a frock-coat with oversize tails, a too-long white waistcoat, too-short black trousers, a staved-in black topper and white spats. A lock of hair was greased down on an otherwise bald head.

The most accepted theory is that the auguste was created by Tom Belling in Berlin in 1864. At the time, Belling was employed by Ernst Renz, a German circus proprietor and a keen rival of Dejean. Renz had a reputation as a strict

opposite right: William Frederick Wallett, the self-styled Queen's Jester, appears at the Alhambra Palace in London's Leicester Square (*Mander & Mitchenson Theatre Collection*)

The Olympic Circus in the Champs
Elysées, Paris, in 1844 (*BBC Hulton
Picture Library*)

disciplinarian. Like many other clowns, Belling had had a very unsettled past.
He had led the life of a gypsy for years and walked across Russia and much of
Siberia with a travelling circus.

He was taken on by a Russian prince at a huge salary to run the stables. After
amassing a fortune he then dissipated it, gambling with diamonds and joining in
the extravagant life of the nobility. He found his way to Berlin, where he joined
Renz to perform as an acrobat, juggler and musical clown.

Renz stood no nonsense from anybody; for falling during a performance
Belling was banished from the ring for four weeks—a serious matter since he
would not be paid during that time. Imprisoned in his room, Belling became a
little bored. Kneeling on his bed in front of a mirror he put on a red wig back to
front; then he donned a coat inside out and—hoping he would not be recognized
—he stole out of the room to watch the circus. Much to his horror he bumped
into the authoritarian Renz. In confusion he backed away, staggering into the
ring itself. He tried to steady himself by holding on to one of the ropes of the
tent, missed and fell over. The crowd mistook his clumsy movements for part of
a new act and roared with delight, shouting, 'Auguste, Auguste!' ('clumsy idiot'
in the Berlin dialect). Renz was only too pleased at the response, and pushed
Belling back into the ring when he attempted to leave. And so, yet another type
of clown had been added to the parade of buffoons which the circus brought
forth—the knockabout fellow with an outrageous red wig and ridiculous clothes
who provides the ever-amusing spectacle of the wrong man in the wrong place
at the wrong time.

Belling later joined the Franconi circus, but his somewhat phlegmatic style
did not suit the Parisians. However, Guyon, who had copied his style, did
succeed at Paris's Hippodrome. Even the prospect of death seems not to defeat

'A Talented Troupe' from the
picture by Charles Green, 1886
(*BBC Hulton Picture Library*)

clowns, and Guyon was no exception. A story tells how, as he lay dying in the
British Hospital of Lavallois-Perret, he was seized with a desire to visit the circus
once more. He dodged his nurse, got dressed and went to the Nouveau Cirque,
where the clowns Footit and Chocolat were playing. The exertion led to a heart
attack, but Guyon died content.

Traditionally, the white clown and the clumsy auguste work as a partnership.
Footit and Chocolat were one of the most famous teams in France. Paris was
enchanted and amused by their daring acrobatic stunts, riding tricks and
tumbling and much amused by their parodies, which depended on plentiful
dialogue.

Chocolat, whose likeness survives in a painting by Toulouse-Lautrec, was a
black auguste. His trade-mark was a bright red cap which he wore to one side of
his head. He also wore a red coat over closely fitting black breeches. Chocolat
was the straight-faced victim of many humiliating kicks, slaps and buffeting.

Footit, dressed in his traditional Pierrot's costume, was the master of the
grimace. He was as well known in England as he was in France, and in 1885 he
appeared in the Grand International Cirque, which was holding a Christmas
season at Covent Garden. A popular piece of absurdity served up by Footit was
his entry, seated the wrong way round on a horse. He would complain to the

141

ringmaster that the horse had no head, at which he was advised that the head was on the other side. 'Turn it round, then', was Footit's retort.

The comic interaction between the white clown and his auguste is known as an entrée. The entrée is not always played by a couple; in the case of the Fratellini brothers it was three-sided. The Fratellinis were sons of an Italian acrobat and sometime soldier under Garibaldi. François, the youngest of the three, was an elegant Pierrot in the commedia dell'arte tradition; his two brothers were his augustes. Paul was the poor little man for whom nothing went right and who was equally upset by Albert, who wore absurd make-up and affected witlessness. The three together were hilarious and so beloved in France that they were accorded a high honour—a performance in the hallowed surroundings of the Comédie Française.

The Fratellinis had begun their careers in the usual way by training as young children in the circus arts of acrobatics, dancing, riding, the playing of all kinds of musical instruments and conjuring. In order to burlesque these skills the clown has to be every bit as good as—if not better than—the serious artist. Once trained, the three brothers travelled the world, settling at the now-defunct Cirque Medrano in Paris. They became popular enough to be able to buy their way out of the contract they had and to perform on stage, in cabaret and finally at the Cirque d'Hiver. For ten years after World War I the Fratellinis were perhaps the greatest theatrical attraction in France.

The brothers gloried in absurd props—not only the outsize safety pin and tiny, ineffectual umbrella, but also bizarre musical instruments, such as the monstrous bass fiddle which would stroll round the ring by itself and the clarinet that turned itself into a telescope.

The Fratellinis were characteristically circus clowns rather than stage clowns. For they themselves, it is said, were not as funny as the antics they performed. A contemporary description of their finale makes this clear:

François bursts into song while wearing a top-hat. Albert sets fire to it. Paul rushes to the rescue with a toy fire engine, rests a ladder against François and mounts it, hatchet in hand. He drives the hatchet into François' head and leaves it there. Albert turns on a hose. François, who has never left off singing, opens his umbrella and marches off with fire brigade in attendance and the hose pouring its ineffectual drip on the umbrella. There has been no attempt on their part to make themselves known to the audience, no confidences, no signals, no expression of emotions, no facial play, not even as much as a wink.

America produced some interesting and completely new clown types which owed little to European tradition. In the late eighteenth century and throughout the nineteenth the great expansion westward and the resulting far-flung communities created a great demand for all kinds of travelling entertainers. For people living austere lives on the frontier, the arrival of a river show or a circus—heralded by a parade—was a momentous event. Also popular were the shows of the ferociously competitive 'flatfoots', so called because of their foot-stamping style of ballyhoo. They began exhibiting animals and later included ring entertainment. There were also sideshows, exhibiting curiosities and freaks, from midgets to bearded ladies, and, of course, the popular minstrel shows.

Wild West shows, or rodeos, which have enthralled audiences since the mid-nineteenth century, also featured clowns. Darting among the daring bronco

142

left: The three Fratellini brothers (*from left to right*) Paul, Francois and Albert, top clowns in Parisian circuses in the early twentieth century, are associated in particular with the Cirque d'Hiver; they are seen (*below*) with their family in March 1924 (*BBC Hulton Picture Library*)

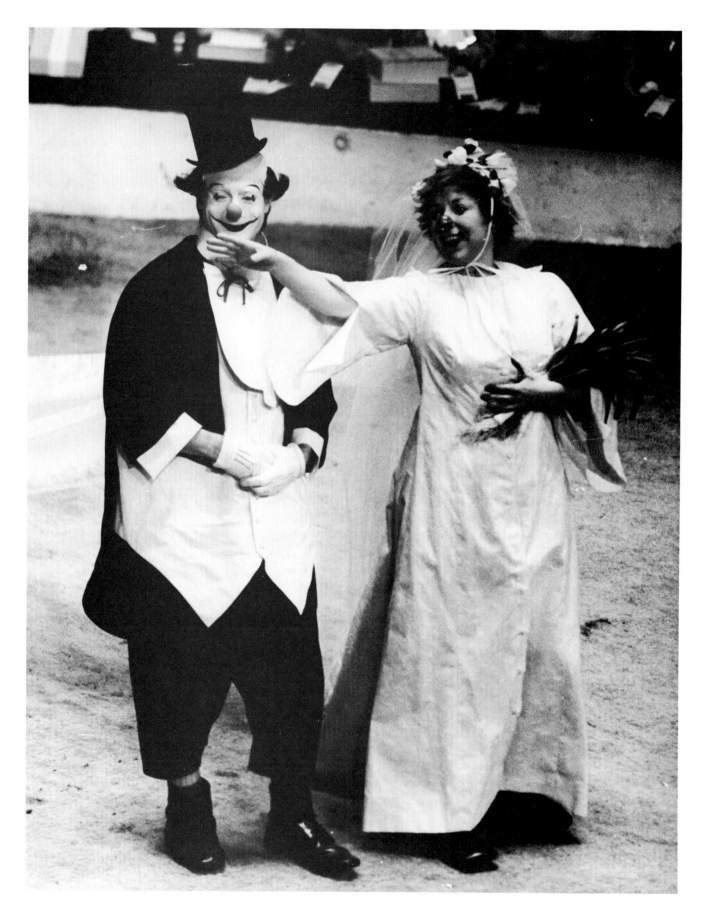

riders, calf-ropers and steer-wrestlers, the clown would be responsible for distracting animals that were in danger of injuring contestants. The rodeo clown also entertained the spectators. He performed in South and Central America as well as in the North. In Mexico the clown appeared in bullfights as well as in the somewhat theatrical kind of rodeo that Mexicans liked.

It was a clown and bullfighter from Mexico who became internationally known to modern audiences as Passepartout in the film *Around the World in Eighty Days*, made in 1956. Known as Cantinflas, he was born Mario Moreno in Mexico City on 12 August 1911. His half-intelligible nonsense patter inspired the Spanish word *cantinflear* which means to talk much and say little. The character created by Cantinflas is a poor Mexican slum-dweller who wears trousers held up with a rope, a tattered coat, neckerchief and an old and dented felt hat.

Cantinflas is also a satirist, and in 1941 he made a film satire on bullfighting, entitled *Ni sangre, ni arena* ('Neither blood nor sand'). He made a great many Mexican films, which made his particular brand of high comedy familiar throughout the Spanish-speaking world.

The first American circus to feature a traditional-style clown was run by an expert horseman of Scottish origin called John Bill Ricketts. He opened his 800-seat circus building in Philadelphia on 3 April 1793. The first performance, which was attended by President Washington, included Ricketts' son and another boy as trick riders and a Mr McDonald as clown. During the circus's subsequent

opposite left: A clownish marriage between Pierre Etaix and Annie Fratellini at the thirty-sixth Union Gala of Artistes, Cirque d'Hiver, April 1969; and (*below*) three generations of Fratellini Brothers: Baba, Viko and Popol (*Keystone Press Agency*)

travels to New York and smaller communities in America, it acquired another clown, a Mr Sully. Sully had been a tumbler and singer at Sadler's Wells Theatre in London. He became very popular—noted especially for his variation on 'The Tailor's Journey to Brentford'.

Another early American circus proprietor was Aaron Turner, who is said to have been the first to use the complete round-top tent. Turner was particularly fond of buffoonery, and his circus included a clown called Joe Pentland. Pentland cracked jokes with the ringmaster, sang songs and introduced a trick not unlike the comic horse riding of Tom Barry. A pretty bareback rider would appear on an elegant horse, which was made to shy at her layers of muslin skirts. A drunken sailor would stagger from the ringside seats and yell that he could ride 'that danged fat nag'. Cheers and hoots of derisive laughter greeted him as he clambered on to the refractory animal, slipped off and remounted. After doffing his outer clothes, the 'sailor' was revealed as Pentland, clad in sparkling tights, and he then proceeded to ride with the greatest of skill.

One original American clown was a man called Daniel McLaren. New York-born McLaren, who took his mother's maiden name of Rice for professional use, wore neither white face nor the seedy evening dress of the auguste. In fact, he wore no make-up at all but grew Uncle Sam chin whiskers which became his trade-mark.

Dan Rice began his circus life as a strong man with a half share in a trained pig called Lord Byron. He has been hailed as one of the greatest clowns the United States has ever seen. After a wandering adolescence during which he raced horses and worked as a pedlar, Rice performed his strong-man act in Nathan Howes' Philadelphia winter circus, in Barnum's New York museum and in various European countries. Rice's first Philadelphia appearance, in 1841, made him an overnight success.

His most popular act was a comic turn on horseback, wearing the stars and stripes costume and goatee whiskers, which had his audience cheering wildly as soon as they set eyes on him. Rice was known as a Shakespearian as well as an equestrian jester and was much given to pieces of doggerel often made in response to questions from the audience or in attempts at getting the better of the ringmaster. Rice was also a notable song-writer; his first popular topical ditty was entitled 'Hard Times'.

Later, Rice opened his own show, in which he worked side by side with Wallett, who had been brought to America by one of the flatfoots. The pair played the river circuit in the warmer months, and in the winter they gave performances at Rice's Amphitheatre in Charles Street, New Orleans, which had been built by admirers. For twenty years Rice appeared in all the river towns, either with his own circus or with others. These were years of great prosperity and fame for him.

The circus was taken to Washington, where Rice acquired a taste for power as he fraternized with Abraham Lincoln, Jefferson Davis and Robert E. Lee, all of whom—in those pre-Civil War days—he counted among his friends. Admirers in and around his home town of Girard, Pennsylvania, nominated the clown for the state legislature, but he did not win the seat. Undeterred, Rice aimed higher; he ran for Congress—hoping to use it as a stepping stone to the presidency—but was again unsuccessful.

Before this episode, Rice's career in the circus had shown signs of decline. He had always commanded high wages, in his prime, in the 1860s, earning an

'Now, if I was Prime Minister . . .'
Emmett Kelly (*BBC Hulton Picture Library*)

astonishing $1000 (£432) a week; and he made high profits out of his own shows. But he spent heavily and irresponsibly, and several times he had to sell a circus in order to pay his debts. He broke contracts with other circuses and drank heavily. However he always bounced back and continued the see-saw of bankruptcy and new enterprises until, at the age of seventy-seven, towards the turn of the century, he died in poverty. Rice's last days were lonely, poor, cynical and embittered, enlivened only by an occasional visit to the big circus in Madison Square Garden to remind him of his flamboyant past.

Although since the 1870s the partnership of the clumsy auguste and the masterful white clown has provided the main kind of comic circus entertainment, another clown type, popularized by the American Emmett Kelly, is almost as familiar. This is the melancholy tramp or hobo clown, based by Kelly on a migrant worker he had once seen.

Kelly began his life in the small Kansas community of Sedan in 1898 and started his career as a trapeze artist at Howes' Great London Circus in 1923. He alternated his trapeze act with a routine as a white face clown, but gradually the mournful vagabond in his tattered business suit and bulbous nose took shape—after an earlier existence as a cartoon character when Kelly was aiming for a career as a cartoonist.

Weary Willie, as the character was called, had circus audiences in paroxysms of laughter throughout America and Europe. Kelly's technique was very simple. Absolutely silent and never changing his sad expression, Kelly would shuffle towards a woman in the audience and fix his soulful gaze upon her face, while at the same time munching a loaf of bread or a huge cabbage. Sometimes, as the audience filed into the circus tent to take their seats, he would seat himself next

The Mexican comic Cantinflas tries to reach the engine of a beleaguered train as it passes through wild Indian country. From *Around the World in Eighty Days (Culver Pictures Inc)*

to an unsuspecting victim, again never uttering a sound. He once described with pride how this act had gone down with British audiences during a season when he appeared with the Bertram Mills Circus:

The Lord Mayor of London was there and I looked out and saw that snooty-looking crowd with their beautiful clothes and I thought, here goes nothing. I was given six or eight minutes and I went up in the seating area, something that clowns had never before done in England, eating my cabbage. I got a tremendous hand.

In his autobiography, *Clown*, which was published in 1954, Kelly sums up his view of Weary Willie:

I am a sad, ragged little guy who is very serious about everything he attempts —no matter how futile or how foolish it appears to be. I am the hobo who found out the hard way that the deck is stacked, the dice 'frozen', the race fixed and the wheel crooked, but there is always present that one, tiny, forlorn spark of hope still glimmering in his soul, which makes him keep trying.

148

Emmett Kelly appeared with the Bertram Mills Circus in the late 1930s after working for the Sells-Floto and Hagenback-Wallace circuses. In 1942 he joined Ringling Brothers and Barnum & Bailey. Ten years later he made his screen debut in *The Greatest Show on Earth.*

On 28 March 1979, Emmett Kelly died of a heart attack at the age of eighty, at his house in Sarasota, Florida. Sarasota is the winter quarters of the Ringling Brothers and Barnum & Bailey Circus, and many of its performers have their homes there. Kelly had left the circus tour in 1956, but he refused to retire completely. He did nightclub acts and made a few television commercials. Each summer at Harrah's at Lake Tahoe, Nevada, Weary Willie delighted audiences during a twelve-week stand.

At about the same time that Kelly made his first film, he was joined at Ringling by another great hobo clown, a contemporary of the famous English-born riding comic, Poodles Hanneford. This was Otto Griebling, a native of Germany who, at the age of thirteen, had been left fatherless. His brother had emigrated to America leaving Griebling apprenticed to a clown and bareback rider. An accident in 1930 left him with both legs broken and he was never to ride again. Undaunted, he taught himself juggling and studied mime while he recovered, in an effort to turn himself into a good clown.

Griebling made a great impression on American audiences. Like Kelly, he wore heavy make-up to give the character an unshaven appearance; his tattered garments and bruised bowler hat could not have looked seedier. His impersonation—of a rather more cheerful vagabond than Kelly's—was created with the help of superlative skill in mime.

Audiences would catch their first glimpse of Griebling as he rushed into the ring and created an enormous clamour by banging two tin plates together. Once he had got their attention, the clown would juggle the plates for a while and then cock his head to one side to listen to the applause. He would cross to the opposite side of the ring and do the same thing. If the applause was not as loud as he would have liked his face contorted itself into an expression of utter disgust. In this way he managed to get one part of the audience competing with the other while in turn they cheered and laughed uproariously.

Griebling was still performing as a clown at the ripe old age of seventy-four. He died two years later, in 1972, basking in the affection accorded all great clowns.

Clowns, incidentally, do seem to live to a ripe old age. There is a charming tale of a Danish clown, Volkerson, who was still cavorting as a comic Pierrot in Copenhagen when he was in his eighties. His frailty prevented him from taking a tumble in the usual way; in a scene where he was supposed to be knocked over, he had to be helped to fall slowly and gently by his fellow clowns. Meanwhile, his loyal audience laughed and cheered their encouragement. Another clown, Charlie Rivels, was still working at the age of eighty-three. A performance at the Grona Lunds Tivoli in Stockholm in 1979 marked his eightieth year in show business.

To circus owners the clown is necessary to break up the tension felt by audiences after a particularly heart-stopping balancing or lion-taming act. The clown lightens the emotional atmosphere, and between acts he helps the audience to prepare themselves for the next moment of thrill and suspense. Sometimes the clown serves a more utilitarian purpose—simply walking around the ring, while outrageously dressed, tumbling and joking, to disguise the fact that the

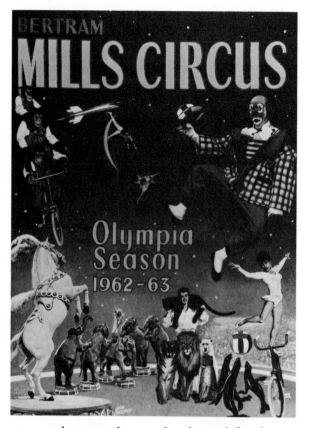

props and scenery have to be changed for the next artist. For the clown, the circus has provided an opportunity for innovation. Freed from the limitations imposed by a script or even a scenario—as in the theatre—the circus clown has a far greater variety of possibilities in developing his act. This freedom also imposes its own discipline: in order to burlesque juggling, tight-rope walking, music-making, horse-riding, tumbling and acrobatics, the clown, as we know, has to be as skilful as the serious artist. The English clown Whimsical Walker summed this up in his autobiography *From Sawdust to Windsor Castle*: 'A circus clown has to knock about, tumble and crack wheezes, and do without properties . . . you must, in addition, be apprenticed to the circus fun, whereas to be a pantomime clown, an apprenticeship isn't necessary.'

But the clown needs more than physical skills. He does not present us simply with the childish comic-strip humour of the man who bangs his nose after treading on a garden rake. He is also telling us something about our human condition. To do this he will need to have a deep experience of life. It seems no coincidence that most clowns have had deeply unhappy—or at least disrupted—childhoods. This early experience of hardship gives them a sense of the absurdity of life so necessary to a clown—as well as the capacity to deal with sorrow in later life. With the exception of Little Sandy, who lost his capacity for clowning on the death of his wife, clowns have shown a remarkable ability to surmount personal tragedy.

The clown's province, according to the Swiss clown Grock, is to make humanity laugh at a picture of its own folly: 'To know what humour is, one must know what life is'.

The clown criticizes us while he amuses us, and nowhere has this been done with more variety than in the circus.

150

9 Three Twentieth-century Giants

It may seem rather invidious to single out certain clowns from among the many, all of whom have learned their trade and given us much to enjoy. But in any of the arts, certain artists achieve greatness; and this century has produced three men who rank among the most inspired and best-loved clowns in the history of clowning. Two of them, Grock and Coco, adapted and improved upon the clumsy auguste character, while the third, Oleg Popov, created an entirely new style of clown whose underlying theme was human dignity.

Sadly, Grock and Coco are no longer with us. Popov, who was born in 1930 into a family of steelworkers in Vyrubuvo, near Moscow, still performs at the Moscow Circus. Here he continues to strive for qualities of realism in his clowning, avoiding the traditional, negative auguste qualities of stupidity, clumsiness and absent-mindedness. Popov is the first truly modern clown, the first to create a positive comic character in which a feeling for humanity rises above the antics of mere buffoonery. He says: 'The chief thing for every circus artiste, in whatever kind of act, is the high dignity of man which must be shown in the ring of any modern circus.'

Popov did not, of course, come to this interesting conclusion overnight. His naive, simple fellow, 'in love with life', who explores realism as well as burlesque, lyricism as well as buffoonery, satire as well as eccentricity, began as a small boy who loved football and had a special fondness for circus clowns. In the cinema, Charlie Chaplin was his hero.

Like most other clowns, Popov had an early life marked by hardship. He was thirteen when his father died, and this, combined with the difficulties of war, forced him to look for work. In 1943 he became an apprentice fitter in the lithographic department of *Pravda*, where he repaired complicated machinery and handled a variety of tools. He had not thought of becoming a clown at that point, but the experience he gained at *Pravda* stood him in good stead later on when he came to make his own circus props.

At about the same time Popov joined a club in the road where he lived called Krylia Sovietov ('wings of the Soviets'), which organized fashion shows, acrobatic shows and air displays. Here, among other schoolchildren, he joined the acrobats and learned to control his body, to walk on his hands, perform on the horizontal bar, turn somersaults and vault. He was ever-mindful of the war—relatives were fighting at the front and rations were very meagre. Popov and four companions toured the hospitals giving acrobatic displays to entertain the war-wounded. The soldiers were greatly entertained and paid them with much-needed food. The fourteen-year-old Popov had been given his first taste of success.

Besides the club, another institution stood near Popov's home—the famous Moscow Circus School. Popov used to watch in admiration the crowds of

boys outside its doors. He felt the same sort of respect for these future artists as he did for a military or naval cadet. The combination of artistry and discipline in their world aroused in him a longing for a 'marvellous but inaccessible art'.

The young Popov was given a place in the school, where for four years he continued his physical training as well as academic studies. In the middle of this period he developed an interest in wire-walking. Secretly he practised in a forest on a wire stretched between two trees, perfected his skill and eventually gave a demonstration to the school. For the first time in his life he had discovered the comic possibilities inherent in balancing acts; it was his now-famous solo comic act on the slack wire that he presented to his examining committee in his final year. The puzzled committee could not find a precise definition for Popov's natural style of humour and matter-of-factly classified his act as 'balancing on the slack wire'.

However, Popov went on to develop his peculiar brand of comedy, first at Tiflis, in Georgia, where in 1949 he appeared in a circus ring act, and later in Moscow, where he was engaged as assistant to the famous Russian clown Karandash. Popov had long been impressed by the older clown's skilful play on audiences' reactions, and it was from Karandash that he learned many of the tricks of the trade—the finer nuances of clowning and, importantly, the difference between burlesque and more realistic styles of comedy. Popov's solo balancing act was also part of the programme.

152

above: This clown, seen on Santa
Monica Beach, Los Angeles, sticks
closely to the auguste's traditions
of red wig and grotesque make-up
(*Colour Library International*)

opposite right: A street musician in
San Francisco (*Colour Library
International*)

After leaving Karandash, Popov performed in a circus in the town of Saratov. There, he had an experience that made him realize his true vocation. Heretofore, he had been a high-wire artist with a comic style. Now he knew that he was to be a clown.

At Saratov, Popov was befriended by the carpet clown Pavel Bororikov. . Bororikov was an old-style, burlesque clown. During one show he had been parodying the acrobats when he fell and was rushed to hospital with an injured leg. Popov had immediately soothed the audience's dismay by rushing into the ring to accompany the clown as he left, burlesquing his fall and lame walk. Asked to take Bororikov's place in the ring, Popov donned the traditional clown's costume and did his best, but he felt uncomfortable, and between acts he wandered around disconsolately. Pushing open a door, he blundered into the circus canteen. Down fell a pile of pots and pans with an indescribable crash and clatter. The cook laughed. But Popov seized a chef's hat, tied an apron round his middle and collected some of the utensils for juggling. He made his way towards the ring and then, by mistake, entered through the orchestra gallery. In the ring he improvised the clown-cook, performing all kinds of gags with his kitchen implements. He was an instant success. Bororikov was watching the performance on the hospital television surrounded by other patients, all helpless with laughter. Popov went on his way to Riga, where for the first time he was engaged as a clown proper.

In 1951 Popov joined a select group of circus performers who provided the milieu in which he could develop his new clown character. This personality was as far from the traditional auguste with exaggerated make-up and ridiculous clothes as it was possible to be. The troupe had been organized in Voronezh by the general directorate of circuses. Many of the performers were former pupils of the Moscow Circus School and they were now expected to build up a programme reflecting 'the spirit of youth'. Among these young artists who were grafting new styles on to old circus techniques were the Boubnov aerialists, the Choubine rope-walkers, and the Abopalov acrobats. They and Popov appeared before the public every day.

The style of the troupe, writes Popov in his autobiography, *Russian Clown*, was 'good taste, *joie de vivre*, virtuosity, dash'. They travelled to Vladivostock, Khabarovsk, Novosibirsk, Kemerovo, Rostov-on-Don, Simferopol, Kostroma and finally to Leningrad. Popov, as carpet clown, made a great impression on his audiences. Among the members of the troupe were two musical clowns, Elena Amrossiera and Vladimir Smirnov. They began their act by driving into the ring in an old crock of a car, which, as circus cars do, broke down at once. As the clowns repaired it, they played a skilful tune using the horn, the pump and various parts of the engine. It is not surprising that Popov thrived in this lively atmosphere. Whether he was indulging in practical jokes or subtly making a point through satire, Popov always appeared in the guise of a simple, happy chap, perhaps a bit soft-hearted and lyrical. He always sought to make his character sympathetic to the audience. Eventually he decided that the red wigs and outsize boots of the traditional auguste were unsuitable to him and did not help put over his realistic style of clowning.

By 1953 Popov had developed the costume that seemed to suit his comic character best. He had recently appeared in a film called *The Ring of the Brave*, in which he wore a broad black and white cap, checked rather like a chessboard. Since that time, the hat has always been part of his costume. His clothes are

opposite left: A Moscow State Circus programme (*Novosti Press Agency*)

slightly eccentric but never grotesque; he wears a slightly shapeless black suit, a white shirt and white neck ribbon. From beneath the flat cap a thatch of red hair sticks out in a wayward fashion.

Like any novelist or painter, Popov keeps sheaves of notes in exercise books. These contain outlines of poses and ideas jotted down hastily during rehearsals or meals with his wife—caricatures, impressions, witty phrases he overhears, even nostalgic verses he composes while away from home. From these jottings he builds new material for his repertoire. By 1957 the notes contained more than eighty different numbers, sketches, farces and interludes, each of which had been performed in public.

Popov never travels without his enormous collection of props, many of which he has designed and made himself. In addition to a telephone, a broom, a doll, a camera and a gun, there are more curious items in the collection: an artificial cow's udder which can be milked, a wineglass which fills itself, a red traffic light, arms, legs and a head made of *papier mâché* and an automatic machine for selling drinks and sandwiches. Popov's live props include a cock, a hen and a small shaggy dog.

While Popov kept traditional elements of naivety and absent-mindedness in his clown character, at the same time he was endeavouring to give him a humane quality and a certain poetic aspect. He felt it was important that the language of the circus should communicate human warmth to the audience. The sketch described below, which was first performed at the World Festival of Youth and Students in Moscow in 1957, will give some idea of what Popov is attempting to do.

The circus ring has been flooded for various aquatic performances. Popov and his sweetheart Lilia stand together on an island inside it. All around them is the sound of nightingales singing—so loudly that they drown out the clown's voice so that he cannot manage to declare his love. 'Lilia', he cries to his love, but the nightingales sing louder than ever. 'Listen here, you nightingales', he cries in exasperation. 'Can't you make a bit less of a noise?' But they simply sing louder still. Then, amid deafening trills, the 'nightingales' come out from behind the bushes, surround the girl and take her away. There he is, all alone. 'She's gone off with them', he says to the audience in a voice full of sorrow—the sorrow of the betrayed lover. He tries to throw himself in the water but is stopped by a clown called Mozel. 'You're out of your mind', he tells Popov. 'What have I got to lose?' he asks. 'It's all over. Once I've made up my mind, I'll stop at nothing.' 'I beg you to think it over', wails Mozel. Swaying at the edge of the water Popov declares: 'Leave me alone, I am going to drown myself.' He takes a rope and ties a big stone to the end of it. Absent-mindedly, he passes the noose round Mozel's neck and heaves the stone into the water. Mozel follows it. Standing upright on dry land, the 'suicide' exclaims, 'Farewell, Lilia!'

Popov's skill in inventing new sketches does not mean that he has dispensed completely with old burlesque ideas. Rather, he incorporates them in realistic sketches, often inspired by current affairs. Targets for satire in his earlier acts included the first Soviet sputniks, the launch of animals into space, modern art, vending machines and the unpredictability of certain types of Soviet washing machines. In a sketch played with one of his clown partners, the fire-eater Iakov Chekhtman, Popov used burlesque to highlight a skit on drunkenness. Chekhtman plays patient to Popov's doctor. Popov suspects the clown of feigning illness and asks him to open his mouth and say 'A-a-ah'. The patient complies,

below: Help! Popov burlesques his skill on the slack wire . . . (*opposite above*) Don't worry. All will come right in the end . . . (*opposite below*) There you are. Nothing to it! (*Novosti Press Agency*)
far right: Popov (in the foreground) during a show at the Moscow Circus in January 1965 (*Novosti Press Agency*)

whereupon Popov produces a huge cucumber from his own pocket and begins to munch it. The implication is obvious to any audience of Russians, for it is the custom in Russia to eat cucumber after drinking a glass of vodka. To underline the impression that the 'patient' is a mere drunk, Popov brings a torch to the patient's mouth and a column of fire flares up.

By 1960, Popov was much in demand all over Europe, but he then became ill with cardiac deficiency. A year later, however, after treatment and rest, he was back at work and toured Germany and the Low Countries. The same year he took the Moscow Circus over the Russian steppes to entertain the people of the 'virgin lands'. Among the clowns was his wife Alexandra, a member of the musical clown trio called Do-re-mi.

Popov continued to include satire in his repertoire during the 1961-62 Moscow Circus season. In particular, he ridiculed 'the lazy and bureaucratic'. A typical satirical sketch was 'The Drowned Man'. This sketch features a callous doctor who refuses to treat a half-drowned man once he discovers the patient lives in a district not covered by him. The doctor serves as a target for any bureaucrat who is a stickler for detail and formality. Burlesque elements in it include a mammoth syringe and a jet of water which spurt from the patient's mouth.

Popov sees his role as a clown as more than just 'comic relief' between the serious acts. This may have been the role of the clown in the early days of the circus, but to Popov clowning has become an act in itself, independent of others and just as valuable as they are. The essential difference between the serious acts and the clown is their different use of eccentricity. Performances of physical acts do things we might consider eccentric—such as walking on a wire—but they do so in order to create positive, heroic characters; clowns use eccentricity to create comic ones.

In Popov's view, a fool must not be such a fool that he is not an ordinary man of the time 'with his simplicity, his irony, his malice and the gaiety which helps him to live and work'. Popov's hero is a simple fellow, in love with life, whose main aim is to create joy, rather than to inspire cruel laughter. Such a character is 'positive, tender, sometimes even lyrical' he believes, and inclines to satire only insofar as it suits his character.

Popov has appeared before audiences in England, France, Belgium, Holland, Italy, West Germany, the United States, Cuba, India, Indonesia, Japan and South Africa. Everywhere his human, realistic clown has received understanding and applause. Among all the superlatives accorded him by the foreign press, one remark in particular seems to Popov himself to express his aims most accurately: '. . . . the laughter he evokes is not stupid laughter, because everything he does has a profound significance.'

Coco was for many years a much-loved figure in Britain's Bertram Mills Circus. His style of clowning could not have been more different from that of Popov. Coco was an auguste—the clown who is always in the wrong and who acts as the *buffo* or foil for the cleverer antics of the white clown.

Everything the auguste does is wrong: if the white clown does a conjuring trick, the auguste joins in and spoils it; if there is anything in his way he is certain to trip over it. The auguste has to grow accustomed to cold water, for buckets of it will be thrown over him; he has to be enough of a musician to play the wrong note at exactly the right moment.

In Coco's heyday, the auguste was often an act on his own. Each clown developed his own style, which became almost his copyright, a style which no

opposite right: Coco the Clown in the early 1950s (*BBC Hulton Picture Library*)

160

Coco amusing children during
rehearsals for the opening at
Olympia, London, of Bertram Mills
Circus (*BBC Hulton Picture
Library*)

other professional clown would have dared to imitate. He often employed
ingenious mechanical tricks, such as tiny parasols which rained, or eyes which
spouted water.

Coco had two distinct styles. In one disguise he would wear an old cap with its
peak on one side, a big and baggy coat, a large dress shirt and collar with an
untidy black tie; on his nose were a pair of steel-rimmed spectacles and under it
was a big walrus moustache. In his other—better-known—role he had lank red
hair which stood on end to express surprise or fear and wore huge boots, flapping
like recently-landed fishes, a baggy checked suit and a red rubber nose. Out-
landish eyebrow arches and a horseshoe mouth were painted on his face.

This familiar figure was the mainstay of the Bertram Mills Circus during the
1930s. His water tricks were a byword, and he once reckoned that as many as
twenty-six buckets of water were thrown over him in every show to get him
wringing wet. A reporter once asked him if he ever caught cold—to which he
replied, 'No. You see, about fifteen years ago I caught a cold and I have still got
it'.

The clue to Coco's deservedly popular success was his love and understanding
of family life. He adored children especially and had six of his own, three of
whom became clowns. Between shows Coco would visit local hospitals and

entertain sick children; he went round schools to give lectures on road safety and judged road safety tests at Saturday morning cinema shows for children. He was made an officer of the British Empire for his work.

If Coco gave love, he also very much inspired it. In 1959, when he was recovering in a Dundee hospital from a motor accident which was severely to restrict his performance, he was inundated with 'get-well' messages from more than seven thousand children. The Mills family seem to have thought the world of him. Cyril Bertram Mills says, in his recent autobiography, that during the many years Coco spent with Bertram Mills he endeared himself to the children of Britain in a way no predecessor of his had ever done.

Although in the minds of the public Coco is always thought of fondly as a British figure, he was, in fact, born Nicolai Poliakoff in Latvia, at the turn of the century, a subject of the Russian tsar. 'I laugh that I do not cry' could very well have been the philosophy of this courageous clown, if the details of his early life are any guide.

From a very young age he can remember longing to work in a theatre. He was actually born in one in Besinowiz, and his father was a property manager in a theatre in Dvinsk. Poliakoff's first performance was at the tender age of five, when he sang and danced like the clowns he had seen in the theatre for the delight of some Russian soldiers in the town's officers' club. At the time his father was fighting in the Russo-Japanese war, and the young Poliakoff's enterprise won him money and food to take home to his hungry family.

By the age of six and a half, Poliakoff was playing small male and female parts in the theatre where his father—who had returned from the war front—was once again engaged as property man. It was while accompanying his father and two of his brothers to Riga, where his father hoped to find work and a place to live, that Poliakoff saw, for the first time, an acrobat. This was a small boy who did his tricks accompanied by an older organ-grinder. Forgetting everything, young Nicolai doggedly followed the pair and pestered them until they allowed him to come along with them. Later, he began to regret this move, but he was afraid to go home for fear of being punished. So he bought a platform ticket at the railway station and boarded a train to Vitebsk, three hundred miles away. There, he eluded the guards collecting tickets and spent the night in a draughty railway shed. Not yet nine years old, he had begun a nomadic existence in which he would entertain in cafés and circuses, often ill-treated by his employers.

The boy was apprenticed for four years to the Circus Rudolpho Truzi, the biggest circus of its kind in Russia at the time. It was the kindly Truzi who gave him the name Coco, sometimes spelt KoKo, which he derived from the similar syllables in the name Nicolai Poliakoff, which the Italian found difficult to pronounce. Truzi gave him the advice he never forgot: if he wanted to be a successful clown, he must first be an acrobat, then a trapeze artist and a tumbler; in fact, he must be able to do everything, and then he could think about being a clown.

By the age of thirteen Coco had completed his apprenticeship and began to prosper in a small way as a trapeze artist, juggler and funny man. The young clown was always a great wanderer. Although this may seem to modern eyes a little wayward, it becomes understandable when seen in the light of a relatively unstable society, and in which, for its starving inhabitants, there was little to lose. After a period playing in theatres in St Petersburg (now Leningrad), Coco had a sudden whim to visit Moscow, and it was here that he was arrested for vagrancy.

The Soviet authorities were not inclined to let a youth wander about freely—he must be placed under some kind of supervision. There followed twelve weeks of utmost misery as with fellow prisoners he was taken many miles in cramped, uncomfortable trains to Feodosia, on the Black Sea, where he had pretended he had an aunt rather than return to his family in Riga. He was cold, dirty, tyrannized by brutal warders, and sometimes even by fellow prisoners. He was eventually given papers which would enable him to travel alone and be released.

During World War I Coco served as an outrider in the Eleventh Siberian Infantry and was awarded a medal for discovering an enemy machine gun in a haystack. He was wounded in terrifying trench warfare and was sent to St Petersburg to recover. There he discovered the humorous camaraderie of the hospital ward and soon found an audience. No doubt his fellow patients were overjoyed to meet this soldier with the wounded feet who at least could walk on his hands.

Coco was discharged from hospital into a city full of the violence, hunger, strikes and armed police which characterized revolutionary Russia. Coco joined forces alternately with the White Army and with the Reds, usually as an entertainer. During this time he contracted typhoid, narrowly escaped execution by firing squad for desertion and learned that his brother had been shot and killed by the Red Army in the garden of his own home. In Moscow he witnessed dreadful scenes of famine. Later, he recalled: 'Even now I cannot bear to think of the hideous scenes of cruelty and hunger and lust that I saw then.' Coco himself was forced to sell his overcoat for two pounds of bread.

In June 1919 Coco married his sweetheart Valentina. Their wedding feast was a pound of bread and one salt herring. With typical audacity, he smuggled his bride into the railway carriage which took him off to fight in the Latvian Army along with fellow soldiers.

After the Revolution Coco gathered together a small circus of his own and toured the Baltic states. Unfortunately, illness and an accident in the ring put an end to the enterprise. He was in the habit of doing a trick in which he caught a samovar after balancing it on the top of a one-legged table. In order to add excitement to the act, he had the samovar filled with boiling water. One day Coco missed the handles of the samovar and was drenched with the scalding water. In hospital his skin came away with his clothes. It took him three months to recover. He could remember the shrieks of delighted laughter from the children in the audience who thought this was the funniest part of the show and how he had managed to make his exit without alarming any of his young spectators.

After this setback, Coco began to prosper, and he gained success in Berlin, where, in the 1920s, he performed for the Circus Busch, then the largest circus in Europe. During a Christmas season in Breslau, he was seen by Willi Schumann, Bertram Mills' equestrian director, and was subsequently invited to appear in the Belle Vue Circus, Manchester. The year was 1929. Coco spoke six languages, but English was not among them. But he left for England with his two eldest children—apparently unimpeded by the authorities—and only went back again to fetch the rest of his family. Except for a break during the last war, when he served with the British Army, part of the time entertaining troops, Coco remained with Bertram Mills for the rest of his life, touring the provinces in the summer and performing at London's Olympia exhibition hall for the winter season. During each performance he would run into the audience and give a

opposite right: Coco in his later years at Bertram Mills Circus. He carries the Belisha beacon which became his trade-mark when he began to give road-safety lectures to his young admirers (*Douglas Dickins*)

164

motherly looking lady a big kiss, leaving her face covered with blacking—much to the delight of the audience, who did not know that the recipient of this sticky affection was Mrs Poliakoff.

In 1950 Coco published his autobiography, *Behind My Greasepaint*. A road accident nine years later left him unable to tumble about the circus ring and do energetic routines. He was restricted to entering the circus and shaking hands with the children at the side of the ring. Coco died on 25 September 1974.

If Coco seems to have survived the misfortunes of his early life with a happy blend of courage and innocence, the Swiss clown Grock is altogether another matter. Grock, whose legendary blundering with musical instruments lent enchantment to the music halls he performed in, knew how to look after himself. Above all he was a supreme artist. Writing in *The Times* of London, A. B. Walkley said: 'There are clowns and there is Grock. For Grock happens to be an artist and the artist is always an individual. After all, as an individual artist he must have invented himself. It was a remarkably happy invention'.

His performance, which invited sympathy yet indicated triumph at one and the same time, was unique. He waddled on to the stage with a self-deprecating manner carrying a huge leather portmanteau, out of which he pulled the tiniest of fiddles. He tuned this instrument by blowing up a green balloon, which he then held by the neck to let the air slowly out to produce a perfect E. The audience would long to rush to help him as he struggled to right the violin and bow which had somehow got into the wrong hands.

Grock's mastery of all kinds of musical instruments formed the basis of many of his tricks. Earnestly, solemnly and with dedication his hands would race skilfully up and down the keys of a piano. Upon his face, covered with chalky

Grock at the age of seventy-two displays his eccentric attempts to become seated at the piano (*BBC Hulton Picture Library*)

white and red greasepaint, would appear a look of rapture; the hands raced on only to disappear over the edge of the piano, and there was Grock sprawling full-length on the floor.

One of his most inspired pieces of business was to move the piano to the chair instead of the chair to the piano. Like many of his tricks, this was said to have resulted from improvising part of an act which had gone wrong. In this instance, the chair had become stuck in the sand of a circus ring, a mishap concealed from the audience by Grock's sudden inspiration to adjust the piano. In another sketch, Grock would fall through the seat of a chair but would end up playing the concertina with extraordinary brilliance in white cotton gloves.

Underneath his felt pudding of a hat he kept his head shaved. (He wore a wig in private life.) This shining bald dome was used to great advantage in performance. If he—supposedly inadvertently—removed his hat and exposed his baldness for all to see, his long chin and cavernous mouth would tremble with mortification and he was brought to the verge of tears.

None of the clown's traditional booby-traps overcame Grock. He seemed to run into them with a kind of exaltation. Grock describes this aspect of his art as '. . . this mastery by willpower, this transforming the little, everyday annoyances, not only overcoming but actually transforming them into something strange and terrific'.

Grock's progress to the brilliant reputation he enjoyed at the time of his farewell performance in 1954 was not a steady one. Much poverty, danger and disappointment accompanied him before he became the established 'King of Clowns', as he was so often billed.

He was born Karl Adrien Wettach on 10 January 1880, the son of a peasant watchmaker, in the French-speaking part of the Berner Jura. His father was also a noted yodeller, rifle shot and athlete, and he applauded his son's determination to become a clown when—at the age of seven—the young Adrien first saw a circus through a hole in the tent. Adrien was taught music and could play at least seventeen instruments well. At the age of fifteen he toured Switzerland with his sister, who performed as tight-rope walker and acrobat.

There followed a period of great hardship, during which Grock worked as a stable-boy, waiter, cook, piano-tuner, conductor, tutor in foreign languages, box-office cashier, watchmaker, gardener, fencing master and water diviner. According to his own account, he was once even called upon to act as midwife. This event took place when he was crossing the Atlantic. He had just painted on his clown's face for a performance when the ship collided with another one. Grock rushed out of his cabin and bumped into a woman who was so startled by the apparition he presented (as well as by the collision, no doubt) that a moment later he found himself helping her—along with a doctor and a steward—to give birth to twins. His clowning seems to have had the same effect on a certain queen of Spain, who was so helpless with laughter at Grock's performance that she had to be escorted from the scene and was later delivered of an infanta.

The clown name of Grock was first used in 1903 in the Roman arena at Nîmes, France. Grock was then in partnership with a clown called Brick, and together they toured France, North Africa and South America. When Brick married, Grock joined up with a celebrated clown, Antonnet. It was at this point that Grock adapted his performance from the circus arena to the music-hall stage. With Antonnet he appeared in the Berlin music halls, where their act got a cool reception until they adopted a less exaggerated and more sharply defined style, better suited to the stage. Success greeted them in the form of an engagement at the Palace Theatre, London, in 1911, after which Grock appeared almost continually in the capital until 1924. For many years he delighted the audiences of the London Coliseum, whom he found 'wonderful, quick and subtle'. But after a disagreement with Sir Oswald Stoll, manager of the Coliseum, and a dispute over an income tax claim for £4,500 ($10,215) he left Britain with his new Italian-born wife, Ina, vowing he would never return. And he never did.

Grock's style of humour did not go down so well in America. A series of unlucky accidents and illness did not help matters and he found that his clowning was considered too simple for the audiences in New York, Chicago and Philadelphia where he appeared.

If Grock had a favourite audience it was the Spanish. In tribute to Spain's favourite sport, he once decided to stage a burlesque bullfight. The bull which had been acquired for Grock's act was a rather tired one, and Grock knew that the beast would never move once it had got into the ring. As the audience became restless, a courage born of despair gave him the inspiration to pull the animal backwards by the tail. The bull made a sudden bound forward and began to run. It ran more than Grock had bargained for; he had not let go of the tail quickly enough and was dragged round the ring after it. His stove-pipe hat flew from his head as he bounced along. Letting go suddenly, he somersaulted and landed flat on his back, much to the appreciation of the watching Spaniards.

Grock announced his retirement twice before he 'definitely and irrevocably' retired for good. He had formed his own travelling circus in Germany after World War II and it was there, in Hamburg, that he gave his farewell performance on 31 October 1954. Writing of this final appearance, Neville Cardus, the late English columnist, said, 'Timing, placing, and the movements were as finely judged as ever, and the total performance was of an almost unbearable brilliance.'

During his remaining years, Grock performed from time to time on Italian television. In Milan, he fell ill in front of the cameras, but managed to complete his act before collapsing. The clown who had extracted mirth for millions out of the simple props of a wig, a stick of greasepaint, a child's fiddle and a chair without a seat, died at the age of seventy-nine in Imperia, Italy, in July 1959. Shortly before he died he had been awarded an honorary doctorate by Budapest University.

10 Spellbinders of the Silent Screen

The invention of the cinema in the 1890s gave clowns greater scope than they could have previously imagined. Skills learned in the circus, the music halls and their American equivalent, vaudeville, were adapted to the screen. A whole new range of comic techniques became possible, thanks to an 'arena' that could literally be as big as all outdoors and a virtually limitless supply of props.

The incomparable Buster Keaton filmed *The General* on the railway tracks which crossed the lumber camps of Oregon. 'Railroads are a great prop', he once said. 'You can do some awful wild things with railroads.' In *Steamboat Bill Junior*, Keaton's arena was the Sacramento River, and his funniest comic scenes were achieved with a hurricane created by special effects. A 120 foot crane was placed on a barge and used to tear up buildings on the set. Using the same crane Buster got himself hurled around, apparently blown into the sky by the gale. One of Keaton's most famous sequences, in the same film, illustrates the endless possibilities of clowning on a large scale. In it, he stands with his back to a house, the entire façade of which begins to fall in one complete section on top of him. The next frame shows him standing—that familiar dead-pan expression on his face—neatly framed by the attic window.

That stand-by of the circus ring, the worn-out motorcar that behaves in a wildly eccentric way, has proved infinitely amusing on the screen. Here the crazy comedy surrounding the car is extended into elaborate and uninhibited chases. These hilarious car chases, inspired by French farce films, became a Hollywood speciality in the early days of the cinema. From 1913 they featured in the slapstick films of Mack Sennett. Sennett, the ex-boiler-maker who became known as the father of film comedy, is most remembered for the Keystone Kops. This lunatic bunch of coppers tore across the screen pursuing a knockabout course, waving missiles of every conceivable kind, leaving chaos in their wake, all ending in the inevitable crash. The chase and the white make-up used on the actors' faces are reminiscent of a pursuit scene from one of the ancient harlequinades—if somewhat more frenetic. An invariable constituent of these early comedies was a glamorous woman. Also invariable were the twin themes of the exploding of highfalutin hypocrisy and a cheeky opposition to authority—themes as old as comedy itself. In charge of the Kops was Chief Teeheezal, played by Ford Sterling, whose every command was misunderstood or plainly disobeyed. He and the rest of the actors needed to be skilled acrobats to sustain the many tumbles that a ride in the Keystone police transport inevitably involved.

The daredevil antics we see in the early silent comedy films were more often than not performed by the actors themselves, rather than by stuntmen. Film technology had not developed to the extent where this use of a double was possible. So cliff-hanging sequences were performed by the stars themselves and were as real as they appear on the screen. Buster Keaton was, above all, a

opposite left: Charles Chaplin's autobiographical film *The Kid*, 1920, showed life among the poor in London's slums through sentimental eyes. Jackie Coogan upstages Chaplin as the Kid, a younger version of Charlie the Tramp. *The Kid* was the first feature film that Chaplin both wrote and directed (*Finler*)

171

master of action. From childhood he had been a vaudeville acrobat and had a body so resilient that he once broke his neck during filming without discovering he had done so until many years later. Keaton stunted not only for himself but also, where feasible, for his other actors. Harold Lloyd, in his comedy-thrill pictures of the 1920s, also performed many of his own stunts. In filming the peculiar predicaments in which he performed some daring feat, Lloyd often faced a long and dangerous drop. This was particularly courageous in view of the fact that he performed with a disabled hand; during a session for some publicity photographs, a property bomb he was holding had turned out to be live and had blown off his right thumb and index finger.

There is one important facet of silent screen clowning that distinguishes it from that of the later sound comedies—in a word, improvisation. The majority of silent film clowns never worked from scripts. Their sequences developed spontaneously from the very briefest of outlines. The comedy was therefore very much the responsibility of the performer rather than of the director or writer.

Not all directors, however, relied simply on the ability of a bunch of comic actors to improvise funny situations. A great rival of Sennett, Hal Roach, whose stable of funny men included Stan Laurel and Oliver Hardy as well as Harold Lloyd, always made sure that his films had a solid plot. However, the sequences were not tightly scripted and there was still plenty of room for spontaneous clowning. The only writers who had any importance in the silent era were the gag writers, who were employed to think up ideas for visual comedy. When Harold Lloyd set up his own company, he employed as many as ten at a time. The innocent baby-faced comedy of Harold Langdon was, to a great extent, their creation. The written gag often served as an inspiration to the geniuses of the silent screen and helped them project their individual comic personalities. Today's detailed scripting and planning—not to mention tightly-controlled

left: The father-and-son musical
auguste team Noe Noe and Gary
clowning at the Circus World
Championships, Clapham Common,
London, in 1977 (*Nick Birch*)

opposite above: French-born Charlie
Cairoli was a familiar and much-
loved figure in Britain until his
death at the age of seventy on 17
February 1980. He is pictured
with his son Charlie Cairoli Junior
at the Blackpool Tower Circus; his
great respect for audiences and love
of children won him popularity
there for almost forty years (*Nick
Birch*)

opposite below: A clown in Balbao
Park, San Diago, California (*Daily
Telegraph Colour Library: photo by
Len Rhodes*)

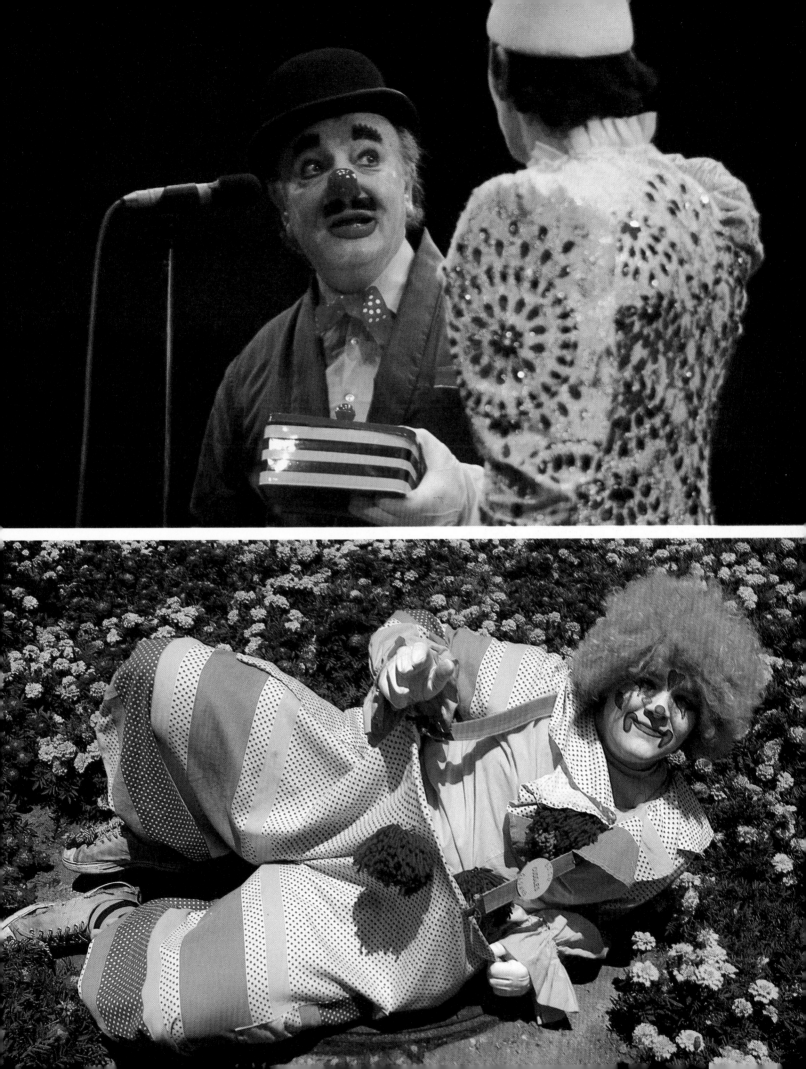

budgets—leaves little space for that special kind of unselfconscious, improvised humour which turned many silent comedy films into classic art.

One of the few clowns who did not employ gag writers was Charles Chaplin, who began making his name in films in 1914, acting for Mack Sennett. Chaplin enhanced Sennett's comedy with his own subtle vocabulary of comic inventions which he had learned in the hard school of the English music hall. A particular device of his was the plank or ladder carried on the shoulder. When the clown turned round, the object would inadvertently smack his adversary in the eye and knock him over. In *The Pawnshop*, Chaplin's innocent weapon was a cello, which had somehow become wedged over his head so that he was unable to see; havoc followed his every move.

Chaplin took Sennett's films away from frenzied knockabout and in its place gave the world a recognizably human character. His poor but jaunty tramp is perhaps the most familiar and best loved clown in the world. He is an irresistible mixture of pathos and slapstick, an unlikely hero who always outwits a bigger opponent and usually ends up with the glamorous girl.

Chaplin's superb artistry was admired and imitated by funnymen all over the globe; screen comics of the time, such as Lloyd and Langdon, began their careers by copying it. A Spanish circus performer, Charlie Rivels, devised a comedy trapeze act dressed as the little tramp. Doug Ashton in America was a celebrated Chaplin imitator, as was Charlie Bale in England. Even the Japanese had their own film version. But most lacked the element of human warmth which gave Chaplin's character his international and lasting appeal.

Although Chaplin never worked in a circus, his tramp disguise links him to traditional circus clowning. The absurd contrasts which the circus clown employs are seen in the incongruity of the tiny bowler and the big, flapping shoes, the tight dinner jacket and the huge, baggy trousers (the originals were said to have belonged to Roscoe 'Fatty' Arbuckle). Charlie looks the epitome of a fellow on his uppers until we catch sight of that dashing cane. Suddenly the downtrodden figure has a debonair and gentlemanly look about him. The cane is his hope, his courage.

Chaplin first created his tramp while working for Mack Sennett. But after making thirty-five films in one year at that studio, he felt that Sennett's films did not allow him room to develop his characterization. In company with Fatty Arbuckle and others, he moved to Essanay and then to Mutual, where he perfected the amalgam of pathos and comedy we know so well. The inspiration for the tramp was said to have been the bemused dandy portrayed by the widely acclaimed film comedian, Max Linder, who made films for Charles Pathé in France before World War I.

Charles Chaplin was born on 16 April 1889, into great poverty in London's East End. In *My Autobiography*, Chaplin fondly recalls his early life with his mother, a soubrette on the variety stage until she was stricken with ill health. Chaplin was one year old when his father deserted the family. He was an entertainer in the music-halls, which in those days were often attached to pubs. The good wages paid to music hall performers reflected the expectation that the performers would inevitably spend a lot of money at the bar. Chaplin's father was no exception; tragically, his addiction to alcohol killed him by the age of thirty-seven.

Meanwhile, Hannah Chaplin had been struggling alone to support Charlie and his elder brother Sydney with her performances. Misfortune again struck the family when her voice became impaired, but it was this very affliction which gave

opposite left: When there is a lot of water and mess about clowns can perform their slapstick routines in overalls and still be funny. Pictured here at Blackpool Tower Circus in 1977 are Charlie Cairoli and Charlie Cairoli Junior (on the ladder) (*Nick Birch*)

right: Chaplin in *The Pilgrim*, 1923, and (*below*) a tranquil moment in *The Gold Rush* the 1925 film Chaplin most wanted to be remembered by. He plays a prospector in the Alaska gold rush of 1898, beset by fellow prospectors who are all greedier and, of course, bigger than he is. The film contains some of the clown's most famous comic scenes: the dance of the bread rolls, the 'meal' of a shoe and its bent nail wishbone and shoelace spaghetti, as well as the log cabin teetering precariously on the edge of a precipice (*Culver Pictures Inc*)

the five-year-old Chaplin his first chance to clown. While she was still performing, his mother usually took him to the theatre at night rather than leave him alone in their shabby, rented lodgings. One night she was performing at a theatre in Aldershot, the site of an army base. It was a grubby, mean theatre, catering mainly for rowdy soldiers. Chaplin was standing in the wings when, in the middle of a song, his mother's voice cracked and went into a whisper. The audience began to sing falsetto and make catcalls. Hannah left the stage. The youthful Chaplin was led on to the stage in her place and sang a well-known song of the time called 'Jack Jones'. Half-way through the ditty a shower of money poured on to the stage. Immediately Charlie ceased singing and announced that he would pick up the money first and sing afterwards. There was much laughter at this. The stage manager came on with a handkerchief to help the small boy gather up the coins, but Charlie suspected that he was going to keep the money and anxiously followed him off-stage. Not until the cash was delivered safely into Hannah's hands did Charlie return to sing. In all innocence, he began to do imitations of his mother singing her Irish march song and even copied the

cracking of her voice. Laughter, cheers and more money greeted Charlie and he was carried off the stage by his mother to tremendous applause. It was his mother's last performance, his first.

Charlie's mother took in needlework to help support her two sons. Then her failing health forced her to give this up and with her children she entered the Lambeth workhouse. From there Charlie and his brother Sydney were transferred to the Hanwell School for Orphans and Destitute Children, where they quickly learned what it meant to be a member of what Chaplin himself later termed the 'mendicant class', at the mercy of the self-righteous. Their education in this uncompromising institution lasted eighteen months. A second spell in the Lambeth workhouse proved too much for Hannah. Exhausted by the attempt to keep her family's heads above water, she went insane and had to be committed to an asylum. She later recovered enough to look after her children once again, but not before Charlie had had a taste of what life under the custody of his drunken, brawling father was like.

Poverty, constant hunger and street fighting, which the young Charlie learned to cope with in real life, appeared later as themes in some of his films. One of these was *Easy Street*, a celebrated short made in 1916 during his extraordinary creative period at Mutual. In one scene Charlie, turned policeman, is called by a local mission girl to help a starving family in the slums. Comically, he scatters food at the innumerable children there in the manner of feeding chickens! Another, more famous, hunger scene appears in *The Gold Rush* (1925). Charlie, as the lone gold prospector in a cabin in the Klondike, becomes so hungry that, with apparent relish, he eats his boots, pretending that the laces are spaghetti, the sole a succulent steak.

Charlie and his brother were right when they decided that the only way to rise above their pitiful circumstances was to go on the stage. They already had a number of stage contacts, and through them Chaplin joined the Eight Lancashire Lads, a travelling troupe of clog dancers directed by a Mr Jackson. It was with this troupe that Chaplin learned that sparkling grin which would later suddenly illuminate the face of his tramp. The Lancashire Lads visited two and sometimes three music halls at night. If any of the young dancers began to look a little weary or bored, Mr Jackson, watching from the wings, would point to his face which wore an emphatic grin. Immediately, the lads were galvanized into a display of happy expressions.

During this time Chaplin had the advantage of watching and working with Marceline, the great French clown. At Christmas the troupe was engaged to play cats and dogs in pantomime at the London Hippodrome, then a new theatre which combined music hall with circus. The sunken floor of the ring was flooded with water. Marceline, dressed in sloppy evening dress and opera hat, entered with a fishing rod, sat on a camp stool, opened a large jewel case and baited his hook with a diamond necklace. He cast his line into the water and waited. After a while, he added smaller pieces of jewellery to the hook, threw in a few bracelets and eventually emptied the whole case. Suddenly he would get a bite and throw himself into paroxysms of comic gyrations struggling with the rod, eventually pulling out of the water a trained poodle who imitated everything Marceline did.

Marceline's comedy was droll and charming and London went wild over him. The young Chaplin performed with the great clown as a cat which Marceline was supposed to trip over. Other influences on Chaplin were Dan Leno and two comedy trapeze clowns called the Griffiths Brothers. Leno was an English character comedian whose whimsical delineations of London's lower classes Chaplin found most endearing.

Besides dancing and observing clowns at work, Chaplin was learning other tools of the trade. For hours he would practise juggling with four tin plates and rubber balls. After a series of odd jobs, Charlie, with his brother Sydney, joined the cast of *Sherlock Holmes* for a tour of forty weeks. He was then aged twelve-and-a-half, but owned to fourteen. Later Sydney joined a group of knockabout comedians. At this time, there were several of these troupes touring the music halls. Although they played slapstick comedy, they were accompanied by beautiful ballet music. They were very popular. One of the most outstanding of these troupes was run by a comedian and former acrobat called Fred Karno. From a repertoire of a few successful sketches, Karno had built a theatrical enterprise of more than sixty companies which produced Christmas pantomimes and elaborate musicals. After joining Karno's troupe Chaplin enjoyed great success in a slapstick sketch called 'The Football Match'.

In this sketch Chaplin entered with his back to the audience, a technique of his own invention. From the back he looked immaculate, dressed in a frock coat, top hat, cane and spats, the epitome of a typical Edwardian villain. Then he turned to face the audience, showing his red nose. There was a laugh; the audience was on his side. Chaplin shrugged melodramatically, snapped his fingers and veered across the stage only to trip over a dumb-bell. Then his cane

The young Buster Keaton in vaudeville with his parents Joe and Myra. Although Buster is smiling here, it was not long before he discovered that a straight face raised most laughs (*Culver Pictures Inc*)

became entangled with an upright punchball which rebounded and slapped him in the face. He swaggered and swung, hitting himself with his cane on the side of his head. The audience roared their appreciation. Chaplin felt he could hold the stage for five minutes without uttering a word. In the midst of his villainous strutting his trousers began to fall down. He had lost a button. He began looking for it, picked up an imaginary object, and indignantly threw it aside saying, 'Those confounded rabbits!' Another laugh followed when his fellow comedian Harry Weldon was due to perform. Chaplin dramatically grabbed Weldon by the wrist and in a stage whisper said, 'Quick, I am undone. A pin'. All this was ad lib and unrehearsed. Both were a tremendous success, and within a few days Chaplin had signed a contract with Karno. He became a leading comedian with the company and was taken on by Karno's American enterprise. He travelled to America as the company's principal comedian in a sketch on secret societies called 'The Wow-Wows'. Chaplin's pathway to fame as the screen's greatest clown was open.

Buster Keaton's contribution to film clowning—undervalued, in the opinion of many critics—was entirely different from Chaplin's. Whereas Chaplin's genius hung on his use of characterization, Keaton's brilliant comedy depended very much on the mechanics of film making. He was fascinated by the details of setting up a visual gag, which he planned with great precision and ingenuity. Many of Keaton's comic moments arise out of his deep knowledge of editing and cutting. We can see how this worked on film in the 1924 comedy *Our Hospitality*.

Buster Keaton and Fatty Arbuckle in *Good Night, Nurse*, 1918. Although Arbuckle never appeared again in front of the cameras after his involvement in a scandal in 1921 in which a girl died, he directed a few films under the name of 'Will B. Good' (*Culver Pictures Inc*)

The film tells a tale of Southern feuding. At one point Keaton is chased by a member of the enemy clan. Marooned on a ledge, he is thrown a rope by his pursuer who has tied the end of it round his waist. Buster secures the other end of the rope round his own middle and waits to be pulled to safety. Suddenly Keaton comprehends that he is now a prisoner and is facing the barrel of a revolver. He pulls on the rope and sighs with relief as the figure of his attacker hurtles past him, perhaps to his death. His expression changes to one of resigned hopelessness as he realizes the same fate also awaits him. The last shot shows the two bodies roped together and hurtling downwards towards the presumed safety of water. The alternation of close-ups and long shots—which suddenly reveal the horrible truth of the situation—is employed here to great comic effect.

In his autobiography, *My Wonderful World of Slapstick*, Keaton says that if he had not been a film comedian he would have liked to have been a civil engineer. In fact, in his portrayal of the little man struggling against enormous objects and machines, Keaton had to solve problems which would puzzle any engineer. In *The Boat*, a 1921 two-reeler, he was meant to launch a craft which he had built and which would then immediately sink. It took him three days to discover a way to make the vessel sink quickly and smoothly and to get the gag on film. Keaton's appetite for the comic possibilities of things mechanical is shown to good effect in *The Navigator*, made in 1924. As Rollo, the rich playboy adrift on a raft with his sweetheart, Keaton creates an immense machine with an intricate system of levers and pulleys whose function is to produce a simple breakfast.

Keaton's superlative skill as an acrobat played an important part in his comedy, which depended mainly on the idea of a puny innocent who becomes a hero, pitting himself against stupid villains, giant machines and forces of nature. He developed this acrobatic skill early in life; by 1900, at the age of five, he was an accomplished performer in his parents' travelling medicine show. Joseph Hallie Keaton and his wife Myra travelled with their son as 'The Three Keatons'. They had worked out a routine in which Buster annoyed his parents and was tossed all over the stage, rarely getting hurt, displaying his natural talent for tumbling and acrobatics. Intuitive artist that he was, the young Keaton learned that he got more laughs if he did not show how much he was enjoying the horseplay. Here was the origin of that uncanny poker face which was later so much a part of his film comedy. The name 'Buster' was given him by the show's escapist, Harry Houdini, later to be known as the Great Houdini. The six-month-old Keaton, born Joseph Francis, had taken a tumble down a flight of steps. Astonishingly—but, as it turned out, typically—the child was unhurt. Houdini picked him up and said to the worried parents, 'My! That's some buster your baby took'. 'Buster' seemed an appropriate nickname for this tough little trouper, and from that moment it was the name by which he was always known.

Keaton had a thorough grounding in comic routines and acrobatics during the troupe's seventeen-year career, which took in Broadway and a job with the 'Greatest Show on Earth', founded by P. T. Barnum—a combined museum, menagerie and circus. Audiences thronged to see variety acts, freaks and monstrosities and also 'The Three Keatons', who were making a name for themselves. The rough nature of the act drew the attention of child welfare reformers, who accused Buster's father of mistreating him. As a result the six-year-old Buster spent his one and only day at school. But his comic sense was so ingrained that he ad-libbed and wisecracked throughout the lessons and was sent home by an angry schoolmarm with a note to his parents begging them never to send their son

Keaton plays a cinema projectionist in *Sherlock Junior*, 1924, and dreams he is in the films he screens. In 1959 Keaton was awarded a Special Academy Award for his 'unique talents which brought immortal comedies to the screen' (*Finler*)

183

Go West, 1925, contains many of
Keaton's most unusual and delicate
characterizations and is widely held
to be one of his funniest films
(*Culver Pictures Inc*)

to the school again. What education Keaton received was given him by his mother.

But the reformers eventually had their way, and it became harder and harder
for 'The Three Keatons' to perform. A trip to England proved unsuccessful;
English audiences disapproved of the violence of the act. The family returned
to America, but the difficulty of getting bookings and Joe Keaton's heavy
drinking led in the end to the breakup of the family and of the act. Keaton made
his way to New York, where he hoped to make his name on Broadway. Instead,
he ran into an old friend from his vaudeville days, Lou Anger, and was invited
to the Colony Studio in Hollywood. There, he met Norma Talmadge, her sister
Constance and Fatty Arbuckle, who was about to begin shooting a comedy
called *The Butcher Boy*. Keaton was immediately fascinated by film making and
began at once hungrily asking a thousand and one questions about technique.
For a year he had a fruitful association with Fatty Arbuckle, who gave him a
sound training in film making under the aegis of Mack Sennett.

America's entry into World War I interrupted his career, and he was drafted
into the army. He spent almost a year in uniform, seven months of it in France,

although he never got near enough to the German army to fight. He returned home to Hollywood in 1919, and for three years, under the management of the producer Joe Schenk, was blithely happy directing his own films. But the big business interests which had such a stranglehold on the making and distribution of films were to be Keaton's downfall. Instead of working for himself, as Chaplin had eventually done under the umbrella of United Artists, Keaton agreed to a deal made by Schenk, who was now also his brother-in-law, and went to work for a company that was to become the giant Metro-Goldwyn-Mayer.

From all accounts, Keaton became the company's property and although he was active in films right up to his death in 1966 he never enjoyed the same personal control over his work that he had had in that brief period in the early 1920s. A revival of his silent masterpieces in the 1950s showed there was still a huge appreciation of his art. Audiences still warm to his portrayal of a man in a hostile world—a world which he only barely comprehends, yet can come to terms with, and which he defeats almost by chance.

Nearer to Chaplin in spirit was the film clown Harry Langdon. Langdon's film character has a similar dignity and pathos without the tramp's worldliness. In place of Chaplin's roguishness and cheeky aggression Langdon offered a hesistant, child-like trust in a world where the grosser appetites existed but were something to hide from. He was, said a colleague, a 'virtuoso of flitting, hesitant motions'. The timid, half-raised wave of the hand typified the innocence of the Langdon character. This character was, according to some writers, less the creation of Langdon himself than of his gag-writer and director Frank Capra, later famous as the director of *Mr Deeds Goes to Town* and *It Happened One Night*. This is how Frank Capra analyses the secret of Langdon's rise from a small-time comic in vaudeville and the circus to a world-famous 'name':

> Langdon himself was at heart a child in real life. Now a child can be bratty, whiny, sulky, cruel. We gave the character the 'fix' that made him appealing —a grown man with the actions and reactions of a trusting *innocent* child. Little babe, least of all, among the legs of enemies tall . . . Langdon *trusted* his way through adversities, surviving with the help of God or goodness.

Before Langdon's meteoric rise in films, he had worked in the circus ring, in a travelling medicine show and as a prop man in vaudeville; he had also been a newspaper cartoonist. With his wife Rose he had performed a comedy car act, in which he wore the soft, short-brimmed hat, long coat and outsize shoes which were to become so familiar to his film fans. Born into dire poverty in Bluffs, Iowa, in 1884, Langdon was almost forty when he appeared in his first film, directed by Mack Sennett. It was based on his vaudeville act and called *Harry's New Car*. His best films were *Tramp, Tramp, Tramp*—based on the vogue for cross-country walking races—*The Strong Man* and *Long Pants*, made in 1926 and 1927.

Whereas the double-take had become *de rigueur* in comedy films of the time, Langdon went further and convulsed audiences with his treble-take. In *Tramp, Tramp, Tramp*, he jumps over a high fence to avoid a rampaging herd of sheep and is caught on a nail in the fence by his high-buttoned coat. Only the audience can see that the nail has saved him from a drop of many hundreds of feet to a busy road below. Dangling in mid-air, Harry frantically tries to free himself. Then he looks down. The sight of the busy road far below makes no impression

Harry Langdon: baby-faced and apprehensive, Langdon sets out to seek fame, fortune and adventure in *Tramp, Tramp, Tramp*, 1926 (*Culver Pictures Inc*)

on him. He tears loose the bottom button of his coat and drops down until he is held by a single button. Disgusted with his failure to free himself, he throws another glance downwards. Still not recognizing the danger he is in, he redoubles his effort to free himself. Slowly the facts of his situation filter through to his dim wits and he freezes. Terrified, he grabs hold of the nail. Off comes the button and the nail begins to bend . . .

There is no doubt that Langdon's brilliant skill as a mime contributed greatly to his enormous success. Nevertheless, when he parted company from Capra, his career went downhill. He took on the help of writer Arthur Ripley, whose talents were not so well equipped as Capra's to show the vulnerable Langdon character at its best. But Langdon, like Keaton, did make a subsequent contribution to film comedy by becoming a gag-writer himself for other actors' films. The best of the films Langdon made can be placed alongside the classics of Keaton, Chaplin and Harold Lloyd.

Harold Lloyd's screen persona also relied on the comedy of the shy innocent abroad who wins against all odds. But his character did not have that strong element of eccentricity present in other screen comics. He portrayed a nice, normal boy, instantly recognizable as a member of the wholesome American middle class. To emphasize this quality Lloyd wore horn-rimmed spectacles. He later referred to the films he made in this character during World War I as his 'glass pictures'. In his 1928 autobiography *An American Comedy* he says that

opposite left: Alma Bennett and Harry Langdon in *Long Pants*, 1927; and (*below*) Harold Lloyd a skilled stuntman, performed his film gags without the use of a double. The scene here from *Feet First*, 1923, was almost as perilous as it looks (*Culver Pictures Inc*)

the character was typical of the time and place, 'assuming that he was moderately poor, that his folks moved a great deal, and that he worked for his spending money at any job that was offered'.

It is said that Lloyd himself did not have an innate funniness. He certainly did not have the early comic training of other silent screen clowns. But one thing is indisputable: the comedies which he made were enormously successful. His film career had begun with an imitation of Chaplin in the form of a comic character he called 'Lonesome Luke'. Tiring of imitation, Lloyd decided to create an individual character which was entirely different. The straight make-up and glasses which adorned his new comic figure were inspired by a film he had seen in which a timid, bespectacled clergyman was transformed into a he-man to be reckoned with whenever justice needed to be championed. *Over the Fence*, made in 1917, was the first picture Lloyd made in which his mild-mannered and optimistic character appeared.

The humour lay in situations rather than in the character himself. This was where his numerous and highly-paid gag-writers came in. Throughout the films gags were interspersed to raise laughs, and gag-writers, actors and directors would sometimes work for days to get an effect they considered the funniest.

At first a Chaplin-imitator, Harold Lloyd developed his own screen character with the adoption in 1917 of a straw hat, horn-rimmed spectacles and conventional clothes. During the following two years Lloyd made 100 shorts, after which he became the first of the silent film clowns to produce features. This scene from *Why Worry?*, 1926, could come from any circus ring (*Finler*)

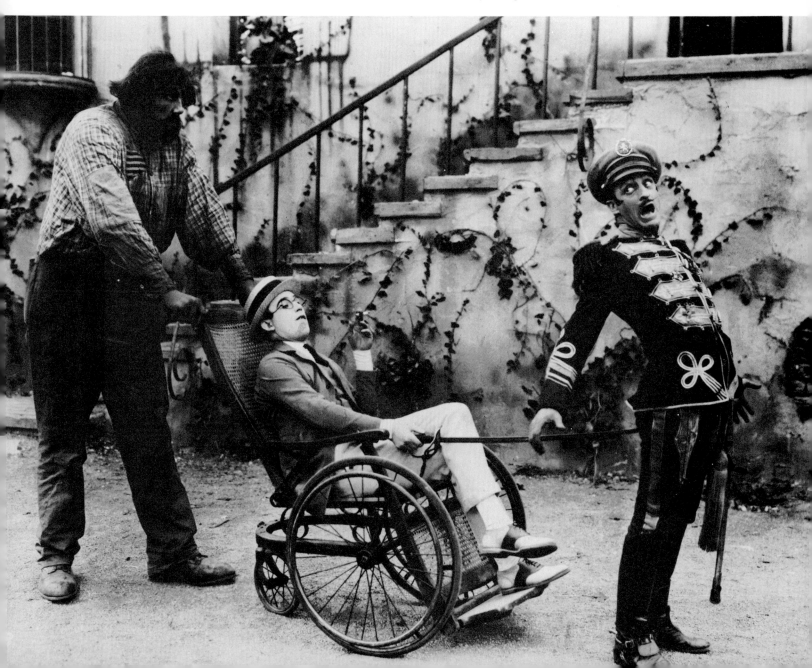

above: London-born Stan Laurel
manages to look above it all, while
his American partner Oliver Hardy
points accusingly in the 1928 film
You're Darn Tootin' (*Culver Pictures
Inc*); and (*left*) Laurel and Hardy
in *Pack Up Your Troubles*, 1932
(*BBC Hulton Picture Library*)

However, the direction and comic timing which made these films remarkable were wholly the responsibility of Lloyd. Like other silent comedy directors, he did not work from a detailed script; the film was improvised from a basic story and built up freely as production progressed. Sometimes the finished result would differ entirely from the original idea. Standard comic elements such as the chase were always an integral part of the story.

Lloyd was the first of the screen clowns to make long features. Coming up behind him in two-reelers were the unforgettable Laurel and Hardy, the modern version of the *zanni* of the commedia dell'arte. The comic whimpering foolishness of Stan Laurel, a product of the British music halls, was the perfect foil for the blustering exasperated American Oliver 'Babe' Hardy, whose memorable catch-phrase was, 'Here's another fine mess you've got me into!' The Laurel and Hardy comedy *Big Business* is considered one of the best and funniest of the silent screen masterpieces—even better than the team's later, still very brilliant, sound pictures.

There is a misguided notion that clowning is for the entertainment of children rather than adults. To take a look at the comic themes used by the screen clowns is to realize just how wrong this is. In the days of silent films there was no such thing as film censorship. This freedom gave a sophisticated bite to film comedy. Films poked fun at all kinds of subjects: homosexuality, wife-swapping, drug-addiction, religion, politics, war, race, deformity, illness, old age and even death were all fair game. Amid the fun, serious points were often made. To give just one example, Chaplin's successful 1918 lampoon of World War I, *Shoulder Arms*, scored satirical points on the absurdity of this tragic conflict.

A clown's performance in the circus or theatre is ephemeral; it is seen and lasts only in the memory of the audience. Screen clowns never die and are as funny today as they ever were. Thanks to television and revivals in the cinema, the magic of Chaplin, Keaton, Langdon and Laurel and Hardy is seen again by new generations. When Chaplin died on Christmas Day, 1977, a French newspaper announced: 'Chaplin is dead. Charlot will live forever'. Similar epitaphs could be written for all the spellbinders of the silent screen.

11 Masters of Mime

Mime has been described by a modern critic as consisting of a few dafties with white faces climbing imaginary stairs. Woody Allen, that most verbal of comedians, has said that he was never quite sure whether the wispy white-faced figure darting about the stage was spreading a picnic blanket or milking a goat.

Both these responses would be typical in Britain, where the verbal tradition of the theatre is virtually unchallenged. The idea of replacing dialogue with action is a difficult one for Anglo-Saxons to accept, and, in the main, the age-old discipline of mime has been left in the care of circus clowns. However, in recent years the Arts Council of Great Britain has provided funds to encourage the art, and successful international festivals of mime have been held at the Cockpit Theatre in London. But despite the work of mime artists such as Lindsay Kemp, Desmond Jones and Nola Rae, the British, in general, could be said to prefer a robust, fleshed-out sketch with plenty of word play to the 'poetry of silence', as Marcel Marceau has described mime.

In America interest is more lively; some four hundred American universities teach mime and several hundred young people are working to become professional mimes. Among the more notable permanent mime theatres in the country are those of Paul Curtis at the Pantomime Theatre of New York and a Colorado community called Le Centre du Silence, run by Samuel Avital. The American mime clown, Jango Edwards, bases his own theatre in Amsterdam, where he also organizes the annual Festival of Fools. His style is a wild, Rabelaisian mixture of clowning, music and mime which aims, above all, he says, at 'the creation of fun and happiness'.

Some see the interest in mime as indicating a return to the tradition of stage clowning and a corresponding decline in the inventiveness of circus clowns. But while it is true to say that all clowns are mimes, not all mimes are clowns. The work of Lindsay Kemp, for instance, is closer to dance; and although his repertoire includes a celebration of silent film clowns and a burlesque Pierrot, he lacks the two basic things which make a true clown: the creation of an individual character and an indefinable something that can only be described as feeling. Similarly, Samy Molcho, a product of the Israeli National Theatre, Habimah, is described by critics as more of a skilled technician than someone who moves the heart. He is a practitioner of orthodox pantomime and appears solo in the costume of an anonymous clown. 'His face and body', said a critic in *The Times* of London, 'are an empty slate to be successively filled with characters and wiped clean.' Alone, he fills the stage with imaginary aggressive people and dangerous furniture. Like Kemp's, his act builds round the running gag of things going wrong: a bachelor suffers the frustration of sewing a button on his trousers; a soldier who proffers the hand of friendship is accidentally run through with a bayonet.

above: Marcel Marceau (*BBC Hulton Picture Library*) and (*opposite right*) in 1967 (*John Topham Picture Library*)

The twenty-odd mime groups in the world today have one thing in common: their styles draw heavily on the work of this century's most gifted mime clown, Marcel Marceau.

Like the little tramp created by his hero, Chaplin, Marceau's white-faced clown, Bip, is a very human character. This small man, who struggles against the problems by which he is beset, captures the imagination. Marceau is the true artistic descendant of Jean-Gaspard Deburau, whose Pierrot was not simply a valet who was kicked but a man who kicked back. Just as Pierrot came into being amid the social conflicts of revolutionary France, so Bip is a response to the twentieth-century struggles experienced by the common man, whether they be struggles against machines, pollution or war. To Marcel Marceau, the clown is a timeless figure because he adapts himself to every age.

Bip takes his name from Pip in Dickens' *Great Expectations*. He is clothed in white except for a gaily striped dickey; on his head there is a battered stovepipe hat from which dangles rakishly a red flower. Bip is ready to face a world too complex for him; his human inadequacy reveals itself as he plays soldier, tight-rope-walker, lion-tamer, weight-lifter, salesman, sculptor or a misfit at a socialite gathering. Writing in *The Times* of London, Ned Chaillet says: 'If the French turned their artists into national treasures as the Japanese do, Marceau would almost certainly be the first addition to the national coffer.'

The man who reached this pinnacle of critical acclaim began life in Strasbourg on the Franco-German border on 22 March 1923. His father was a Jewish butcher named Mangel who later perished in Auschwitz. As a child Marceau loved to delight his friends with imitations of Chaplin, dressed in trousers borrowed from his father and equipped with an inked-in moustache. Marceau has always been greatly enamoured of the silent film clowns and admires Keaton and Chaplin in particular. Stan Laurel became a good friend of his. (It is an amusing irony that Mel Brooks should have chosen Marceau to speak the one and only word in *Silent Movie*, his celebration of the silent film comedy era.)

With the exception of an aunt who was a ballet dancer at the Teatro Colón in Buenos Aires, there were no members of Marceau's family on the stage. However, his father loved to sing and possessed a beautiful voice; there was also an uncle who sang baritone. Perhaps tongue-in-cheek, Marceau suggests that with these fine voices around him it is little wonder that he himself was reduced to silence. But his first love was for the visual, and at school in Limoges he studied decorative art, specializing in enamelling.

At the age of eighteen Marceau joined his brother, Alain, in the French Resistance. His task was to escort Jewish children and the children of underground fighters to safety in Spain and Switzerland. A year before the close of the war, in danger of discovery by the Gestapo, Marceau fled to Paris. There he went to the Théâtre Sarah Bernhardt to study under Charles Dullin, a theatrical director of genius. Marceau was following in the footsteps of another great force in French theatre, Jean-Louis Barrault, who before him had been a pupil of both Dullin and Étiennè Decroux at the Atelier in the 1930s. Decroux is regarded as the codifier of mime, an apostle of silence. It was his grammar of mime, more than anything, that formed the basis of modern technique.

After the liberation of Paris, Marceau joined the First French Army, the army of occupation. Le Rideau de Feu ('The Curtain of Fire') was the name he gave to the troupe of military comedians he formed at this time, which presented shows to soldiers of occupation in Germany. After demobilization he joined the

Marceau as Bip the Clown. Bip is a corruption of the name of Dickens' hero in *Great Expectations*. A lover of the works of Dickens from childhood, Marceau performed his own version of *A Christmas Carol* for BBC television (*John Topham Picture Library*)

theatre company of Barrault and Madeleine Renaud and increasingly developed his talent for mime. The attention of the critics was soon focused upon him for his role of Arlequin in *Baptiste* at the Théâtre de Marigny. This mimodrama was adapted from the French film, *Les Enfants du Paradis* ('The Gods', the theatre audience in the cheapest seats high up in the gallery), which was the fictionalized story of Deburau.

Bip was born in 1947 in the tiniest of Paris theatres, the Théâtre de Poche. Bip's first audience was a small but select one which included the painter Dubuffet, the writer Paul Guth and the distinguished actors, Pierre Brasseur, Barrault and Renaud. Marceau followed this success with a tour of Switzerland, Italy, Belgium and Holland performing full-scale mimodramas—among them *Pierrot de Montmartre*, *The Matadors*, *The Little Circus* and *Don Juan*. Growing fame culminated in full public recognition with his solo performance at the Studio Champs-Élysées of a mimodrama based on 'The Overcoat', a story by Gogol. It is the tale of a poor clerk who scrapes and pinches to buy an overcoat,

194

enjoys a brief social triumph and is crushed at once when the overcoat is stolen from him. The piece displayed Marceau's singular creation of an original style in which mime responds to the body's inner rhythms rather than employing the classical alphabet of stylized gesture.

It would be easy to watch Marceau perform and simply admire his virtuoso technique—his ability to create illusion in an empty space, his seemingly effortless capacity to lean on imaginary mantelpieces. But this is to disregard the very serious meaning underlying Marceau's comedy. For example, Bip may amuse us by making and fitting on different masks until he almost gets stuck with the mask of laughter; but when he finally removes it he reveals a face of grief. Marceau may enact a man struggling to escape from a cage who discovers that the prison he is free from is within another. The interpretation may be comic, but the situation is serious—as in his drama of a nervous, small David at odds with a huge, bragging Goliath. However insouciant Bip appears, to Marceau he is a personifier of the free conscience of man, which is beyond any political system.

Marceau considers himself a progressive, someone who advocates peace and who has struggled for enlightenment in the world: 'My art has to bring light to man, as a painter does when he has something to say about society, as Goya and Daumier did. I am not just an entertainer. I want to be a man who will represent as an active witness my time, and want to describe without words my feelings about the world.'

Marceau has appeared on television and in films, but it is in the theatre that he particularly thrives. There are two parts to his show: one is the *pantomime du*

above: A still from Marcel Carné's 1945 film of nineteenth century Parisian theatrical society, *Les Enfants du Paradis*. Made during the German occupation, the film evokes the love between the mime Deburau (*below*), played by Jean-Louis Barrault, and Garance, a beauty who also claims the love of an actor, an aristocrat and a criminal (*Finler*)

195

Boris Amarantov (*Novosti Press Agency*)

style, in which he first shows the audience all the possibilities of mime, such as walking against the wind, climbing imaginary stairs, the tug of war. This part of the programme continues with a selection of satirical dramas silently announced by elaborately dressed actors who carry banners in the manner of the commedia dell'arte. The second part contains Bip—who, comments Marceau, 'can sometimes win but is most often beaten down'.

Marceau's fame reached new heights with a tour of America in 1955. His show ran for six months in New York, and he became much in demand by American provincial cities and universities. Later, he appeared before the then president of the United States, Lyndon Johnson. At the other end of the social spectrum, his audiences have included inmates of prisons in Europe and America. Mass audiences were opened up for him with appearances on television on the 'Red Skelton Show' and Rowan and Martin's 'Laugh-In'. His television work in the United States has won him two 'Emmy' awards. For British television

Marceau filmed a mime version of Dickens' ghost story *A Christmas Carol* in a music hall in London's East End.

A theatre in the heart of Paris is the scene of Marceau's latest venture. The Théâtre de la Porte St Martin houses not only an auditorium but also a school, where Marceau passes on the intricacies of his art. The school was opened in 1978 with financial help from the French Government and has places for 100 students, from among whom Marceau hopes to form a mime troupe. His former troupe, the Compagnie de Mime Marcel Marceau, had disbanded in 1960 (after eleven years) because of money difficulties and the pressures of his exacting tours. Now his life is taken over more and more by teaching and directing rather than performing.

When Marceau's energies are not taken up with work, he finds time to relax at his farmhouse in a calmly beautiful village in Normandy. Surrounded by his collections of dolls, toys and masks, many from the Japanese Noh theatre,

Marceau lives with his wife and two young daughters, welcoming occasional
visits from his two grown-up sons. In these peaceful surroundings he paints and
writes. His paintings are highly regarded, apart from their curiosity value as the
work of an international mime artist. He also indulges his passion for trees, and
since moving into the 250-year-old farmhouse he has planted 3,000. A studio,
complete with barre and mirror, has been built near the farmhouse, and here
Marceau, his life's work never far from his mind, practises the techniques which
he has employed with such consummate artistry—an artistry which has broken
through national barriers to speak to attitudes and emotions common to us all.

Marceau's timing and the structure of his performance have been copied by
many of his pupils. But a clown's character can come only from inside him; the
technique is mere clothing. Dimitri, a Swiss clown who studied under Marceau
and Étienne Decroux, portrays an entirely different clown character from Bip.
No inadequacy here; Dimitri plays the role of a naive, curious, child-like fellow
who approaches everything around him with an enthusiastic and innocent
delight. In addition to his mime skills, Dimitri uses the circus techniques of
tumbling, juggling, balancing and contortion. Like Grock, with whom he once
worked in the circus, Dimitri combines his solo clowning with musical eccentricities. He can play a tune by bouncing ping pong balls out of his mouth. As a
railway porter he will perform on the marvellous instrument he discovers in the
luggage he is carrying. He will play a French horn, while balancing it on his
mouth at the same time. Dimitri's early working experience was as a circus
auguste with the experienced white-faced clown Louis Maïsse. But his work
now takes place almost entirely on the bare stage of a theatre. His only con-
cession to the auguste character is a slightly over-large mushroom-coloured
jacket, short black trousers and red socks. He wears the mime's white face
embellished by black eyebrows and black triangles beneath his eyes.

An interesting pair of mime clowns are New Zealand-born Bryan Divers and his partner Matthew Burton from Australia. They are interesting because they combine elements from both the mime and the auguste clown and also because, unlike most mime artists, they are Anglo-Saxons. The pair perform with a Norwegian musician, Patrick Iversen, and call their three-man show the Cacofonico Clown Theatre. In 1974, after touring New Zealand's beaches and holiday places in Auckland's Living Theatre Troupe, Bryan journeyed to Paris, where he studied at the Jacques Lecoq school of mime. He joined forces with Matthew, and together the pair toured Italy for a year and a half, performing in the streets of cities and country towns and in political theatre and workshops.

Their use of mime was at first a way of overcoming the language barrier; but after a tour of Belgium, Holland and Germany, including a month in Berlin, the troupe came to England to develop their show using their native language. The show, called *So It Goes!*, was a mixture of puppet mime, mask and music. Unlike most mime clowns, Divers and Burton wear red false noses and the ill-fitting jacket and baggy pants of the auguste. English audiences proved to be less receptive than the Continental ones the pair had amused for the previous five years. The British are too ready to relegate the clown to the category of children's entertainment, but Cacofonico believe much of their dialogue is too subtle for children to understand. However, children would enjoy the music for the show from which the troupe takes its name; as well as a flute and guitar, it includes pots, pans, tins, hubcaps and other assorted junk. Although Cacofonico have worked in political theatre they do not regard their work as didactic. Their clowning does reflect their own social consciences, they say, but it should be regarded as universal, 'not pertaining to any culture or environment'.

A scene from the award-winning *Private View*, shown at the Thames Television Centre in 1978 (*John Topham Picture Library: photo Lesly Hamilion*)

12 The Clown in the Modern World

Marcel Marceau perhaps sums up the plight of the clown today when he says that snobbery alone prevents a clown from being appreciated like Lord Olivier. In Marceau's opinion, there should be no difference in status between a classical actor and a clown; both are capable of great artistry. Great artistry apart, the two have one thing in common and that is the need for a place to perform.

Traditionally—at least, since the late eighteenth century—that place has usually been the circus. There is no doubt that clowns and circuses need each other. However, the high cost of keeping a circus on the road has led to the faltering, and sometimes the demise, of some of the big-name circuses. Other than in Russia, her satellites and some EEC countries, government support is not always available. In the West, in general, circus arts are not considered respectable enough to qualify for the kind of help given to opera and ballet, for example.

In the late 1970s the situation in France improved when state support was made available for ailing circuses. President Giscard d'Estaing responded to pressure from Christian Boner, President of the French Circus Association, and joined him in expressing concern about the future of circuses. This concern had arisen after the collapse in 1978 of three big French shows; two of them were the Cirque Jean Richard and the Cirque Pinder, both run by Jean Richard, the actor famed for his portrayal of Maigret; the other was the century-old Rancy Circus. Richard has sunk most of his personal fortune into keeping his circuses alive. To give some idea of the enormous amounts of money involved, his shows, combined, cost more than £6,000 ($13,620) a day to keep on the road. Now that circuses in France qualify for aid in the same way as theatre, Richard's two shows are back in business.

In Britain, circuses, bowed down by their enormous overheads, keep going only by penny-pinching economies. In one instance, the circus proprietor Gerry Cottle, 33-year-old son of a Surrey stockbroker, was forced to relinquish one of his two shows just at a time when he looked set to equal the great post-war success of Bertram Mills. Himself a one-time clown and juggler, Cottle was at one period enjoying the satisfaction of presenting three travelling circuses, two in Great Britain and one in the Arabian Gulf. A bad debt and other financial losses meant that he had to cut back ideas of expansion; as a result, 120 circus staff—including three clowns—were sacked.

Cottle is particularly resentful of a government which gives help to small fringe theatres, yet offers no support whatsoever to the circus. He even saw fit to publish his feelings in his 1979 circus programme:

. . . unlike circus in several E.E.C. countries, British circus receives no financial help or concessions from the government. Most other forms of entertainment in this country are subsidized—circus only pays tax on top of

201

right: Lessons in laughter. Professor Oscar Lowarde of George Hamid's Steel Pier School for Clowns, with pupil Billy Rice (*Keystone Press Agency*)

enormous overheads, and on top of these problems the British public, used to mediocre shows for so many years, seem unwilling to pay economic prices to see a top quality show.

The Arts Council, the British Government's arts aid body, has £70 million ($159,000,000) a year to spend; a large part of this sum goes towards the support of Covent Garden and the English National Opera as well as the National Theatre and the Royal Shakespeare Company. The Arts Council has claimed that it has no formal policy about support for circuses. However, money is found to fund community drama, fringe theatres and street performances, many of which use clown and circus techniques. A letter on the subject from Jonathan Lamède, the drama officer of the Arts Council, seems to support Marceau's claim that a certain snobbery exists in regard to the circus and its relation to other forms of theatre.

The Council does indeed subsidize a number of drama companies, including a company which uses clown techniques, which like many other activities are an established part of drama. However, it does so in response to artistic programmes and with regard to proven standards of performance work. The principal aim is to provide assistance towards this work and naturally that helps to ensure the companies' survival. But this last fact is incidental rather than central to the pattern of subsidy.

opposite above and *below:* Charlie Rivels appears with Bertram Mills Circus at Olympia, London, in January 1947 (*BBC Hulton Picture Library*)

202

The Council subsidizes drama performance work and does not provide subsidy for circuses. If circus proprietors harbour some resentment I would suggest that this is based upon a misunderstanding, since it is arguable whether their work is strictly comparable with that of companies currently being subsidized.

The single company using clown techniques which does receive support from the Arts Council is Clown Cavalcade. Clown Cavalcade is a troupe of fourteen ex-actors, teachers and community workers, headed by Brian Dewhirst. The troupe is typical of many street theatres which use circus skills and the burlesque elements of clowning in a dramatic context. The enterprise is dubbed 'children's experimental fringe theatre' for the purpose of the grant, but Dewhirst feels it is much more than this. In addition to entertaining schoolchildren and the handicapped, the troupe's purpose, as he sees it, is to improve the image of British clowning. In order to do this he plans to set up a school for the comic arts in Brixton, South London, in the expectation of support from industry. Dewhirst is eager to keep alive clowns' traditions, such as the painting of clowns' faces on eggs, once used as a way of recording a mask.

Despite the troupe's definition of clowning as 'creative anarchy', members submit themselves to rigorous and formal training. In a church hall in Kennington, the troupe learn mime, acting, singing and dancing. For fitness they practise a cross between acrobatic and balletic exercises. Learning the right way to fall and to execute slaps are other important parts of the training. Musical talent is represented by several members of Clown Cavalcade who play the piano, guitar, flute and concertina.

Following performances in the hallowed surroundings of the National Theatre, Clown Cavalcade was hailed by a Sunday newspaper as the first company to make clowning respectable. But among old-school clowns, particularly those in

Emmett Kelly, America's famous tramp clown, employs his soulful romanticism to bring a smile to the face of a woman in a London audience. The occasion is the post-war return in 1947 of Bertram Mills Circus (*BBC Hulton Picture Library*)

the close and clannish world of the circus, street clowns and fringe theatre troupes are regarded with evident disdain. This attitude is not just a matter of resentment at the government support fed to such troupes; many older clowns feel that street clowns are dilettante—'students' having fun in the vacations or merely resting actors in disguise. Indeed, street clown troupes, such as the anarchistic Rough Theatre, make no secret of the fact that they use clown techniques merely as a means of reaching a popular audience. To them, the clown's conventions appear too narrow and not in touch with what they term 'the real world'. Again, groups which aim to encourage arts in the community will advertise evening workshops in clowning next to soft-toy making and story-telling, a sure sign of an amateur approach.

To be fair, there is no doubting the sincerity of these new-style clowns. Although to a professional clown their performances may seem self-indulgent, they are nevertheless highly imaginative, and they employ satire in a way not seen in today's circus. The conservatism of many circus proprietors, who choose to ignore any subject which they feel might offend audiences, has no place in the street, where—free from all limits except the law—clowns cheerfully poke fun at society's foibles. Kaboodle, one such clown troupe, once brightened a grey London Sunday with a parody of the latest craze for jogging. Calling themselves the City Fits, and dressed in nineteenth-century business suits, they jogged round the West End, amusing spectators with their clownish exercising, opening very wide newspapers as they ran, pausing to become statues and 'stealing' an orator from Speakers' Corner. Among some of the skills Kaboodle learn at their clown workshop are fire-eating, lying on broken glass and beds of nails, and performing various tricks on motorcycles, such as jumping over bonfires.

It is not hard to understand why professional clowns are critical. Many of them will have earned their right to the name 'clown' by doing hard, low-paid

205

Charlie Rivels and Alfredino (*BBC Hulton Picture Library*)

work for many years, helping to get the circus on the move as well as appearing in the ring. Part-time clowns know little, if anything, of such behind-the-scenes labour. In America, the young clowns trained by Ringling Brothers and Barnum & Bailey are similarly an object of suspicion to older, experienced clowns. Thanks to union effort, an untried performer, fresh from the Clown College's eight-week training course, will get paid as much as a clown who has been proving his worth for upwards of forty years.

If part-time clowns are an irritation to many seasoned professionals in Britain, they must have to be an accepted fact in the United States. There, amateur clowns number in their thousands, and strict identity with the augustes, white faces and hobos of tradition has to some degree been lost. An article that appeared in *Calliope*, the magazine of the Clowns of America organization, gives some indication of this move away from professional clowning. The story describes the growing number across the country of groups of young people who learn clown techniques and perform in orphanages and local hospitals. Many of the groups are run by church youth leaders. One, called 'The Holy Fools', is led by an Iowa minister, the Rev Bill Pickum, and has some 1,500 members, most of them teenagers.

Amateurs are not wholly despised by circus people. Many American circuses will use amateur clowns to fill a gap if there is no professional available. In Britain, Colin Parker, a coal-miner from Yorkshire, has spent his holidays performing as the clown 'Konky' with a clown from one of the country's premier circus families, Sonny Fossett. But the main question regarding clowns and their future is not so much whether their traditions should be imitated and diffused by amateurs, but how they are regarded by the show business establishment. The late Butch Reynolds summed up the modern clown's predicament in his 1954 autobiography *Broken-hearted Clown*:

The modern clown in this country [Britain] does not have quite the same standing in show-business as he had years ago. There was a time when most clowns could ride, do the ring or bars, work the trapeze, juggle or present horses in an emergency. Now few of them can do more than their entrées, gags and run-ins, with the result that many proprietors begin to look on clowns as something like the measles that 'you can't help having around'.

This dismissive attitude towards clowns is more a reflection of the high cost of running circuses than a refusal to accept the clown at his face value. Clowns in the circus may find themselves engaged in repairing the bandstand or fixing the engine of a lorry and perhaps doing a little driving, in addition to their work in the ring. If a clown can add other acts besides clowning to his repertoire he will obviously be worth more in a proprietor's eyes. However, this versatility has always been part of circus life and is usually totally accepted by clowns, particularly those who were born into a circus family. It is not uncommon for circus owners themselves to double as clowns if the need arises. Bobby Roberts, of the successful Roberts Brothers Circus, will pit his wits against six frisky lionesses and later appear in the same ring as a clown in a comedy car act.

One of the newer breed of clowns divides his profession into two classes. According to David Lloyd—known as Mr Turkey Sandwich—there are worker clowns and there are artist clowns; the artists, he considers, are very, very few and the brashness of many circuses does not allow them much room.

206

left: Douglas Bickerstaffe, Chairman of the Directors of the Blackpool Tower, visits Charlie Cairoli in his dressing room and (*below*) clowns make-up in their dressing room before going on for the first Christmas show at the Agricultural Hall, Islington, London, in December 1937 (*BBC Hulton Picture Library*)

The sad truth about circuses in Britain is that animals are more profitable than people; if a circus fails, a clown must look for work elsewhere, while an animal act is a saleable asset. The Smart circus family, whose 6,000-seat big top came off the road in 1972, created a safari park at Windsor and in 1977 sold it for £1½ million ($3,405,000). Another example is provided by Gerry Cottle; while he was struggling to keep his circus empire from bankruptcy not one animal was lost.

It may be true that the peak of prosperity that British circuses enjoyed after World War II will not be repeated. In the past the names of clowns were inseparable from the shows in which they performed: there was Pimpo and Sangers, Coco and Bertram Mills. Nowadays the general public will more readily remember the name of a slightly talented pop music group than the name of a clown. Happily, there are exceptions: Charlie Cairoli, who delighted audiences for the past forty years at Blackpool Tower, one of Britain's permanent circus sites, was probably the country's best known and best loved clown. Yet Cairoli's popularity may have had more to do with his numerous appearances on television than with his work as a circus clown. This doyen of British clowns also played regularly in Christmas pantomime, partnered by his son, Charlie Cairoli Junior, and another clown called Jimmy. Here his genius for slapstick and musical clowning was as much in evidence as it was in the ring.

The mime clown apart, the modern stage does not happily accommodate the clown, except in the case of pantomime, cabaret or holiday camp entertainments. The days when Grock drew thousands to the London Coliseum to applaud his

209

two-hour-long show of musical eccentricities are long gone. The music halls and variety stages where Dan Leno and Percy Huxter, that elegant British white face, learned their trade have disappeared. A clown would no longer fill an auditorium in New York, as did George L. Fox at the old Bowery Theatre a century or more ago.

Although opportunities for clowns seem few and many feel that inventiveness has dried up, there is still room for hope. If the big circus names are not around any more, there are still plenty of smaller shows touring Britain of which clowns are a very necessary part. Whereas in a theatre the job of stage-managing is done behind the scenes, in a circus it is carried on in full view of the audience. Cages are dismantled and props removed before the next act can commence. Between the acts, performers—the ringmaster, a pretty rope-dancer in a spangled leotard and especially the clowns—take the audience's attention away from the activities of the ringboys and provide relief from the tension of watching hazardous acts. Carpet clowning is not necessarily to be despised as an inferior kind of clowning. It is an essential ingredient of circus and holds the show together. Like any kind of clowning it can be done impressively or badly. The lazy clown, who may be simply a tent boy in motley, will be satisfied with tottering round the ring tickling members of the audience with a feather duster, or he may use the hackneyed routine of a bucket of water on the end of a pole. But good carpet clowns include a short sketch, often in mime, which in itself possesses great charm. A particularly stylish British carpet clown is Tommy Cook, known as Brum, who enacts a very funny performing flea skit. The better known clowns, such as Cairoli, Jacko Fossett and Jacko's former partner Little Billy, are not above the run-in and consider it as important as their longer entrées.

However, the fact remains that there are fewer and fewer clowns entering the circus world. Clowning takes many years of experience and to established

Young Soviet clown Leonid Yengibarov (*Novosti Press Agency*)

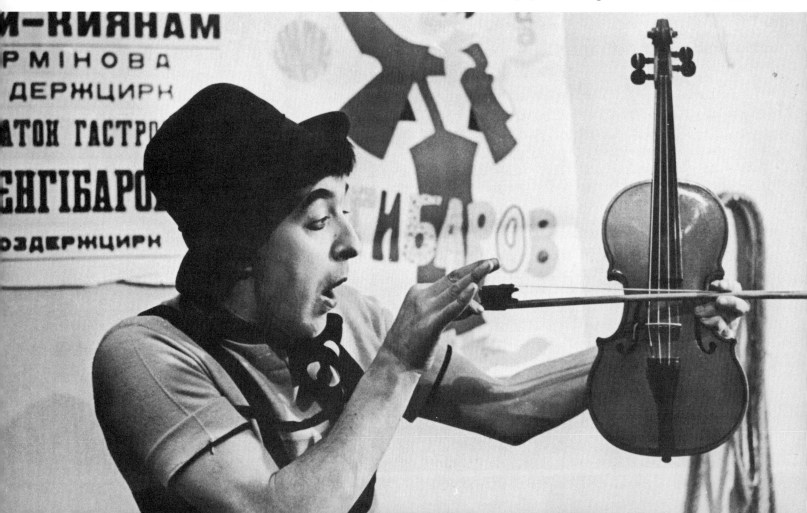

clowns it appears that younger people are too lazy to work at clowning and master its subtleties and traditions. Charlie Cairoli, who, after sixty-five years as an auguste, was in a position to know, believed that the traditional clown would die out altogether if he did not change to suit the tenor of the times. As far as his own act was concerned, he believed that audiences are much cleverer than they were and that to please them even slapstick had to have a built-in logic; there must be a reason for throwing the custard pie. He based his entrées upon everyday, topical situations, for he believed that much of the laughter he got was from people seeing a situation in which they could imagine themselves. Change was important, he insisted. A clown must add something different to his act all the time; people would laugh at it if it had a basis in reality. Cairoli expressed his attitude towards the art of clowning in terms that perhaps only a man brought up in France would use: 'The clowns' traditions have to be treated just as a great chef like Escoffier would a piece of meat. You must not simply roast or boil it in the usual way. You try to change the way you do it to produce something special. That is the way I work.'

Some clowns try to attract modern audiences by borrowing themes from popular television shows, but one British clown thinks this is unnecessary. Rodney Mack keeps clowning alive in the most traditional ways, helped by a natural gift for humour and by being his own boss. In the face of bad weather, rising costs and competition from televised sports events, his family troupe has toured the Scottish villages in the summer for the past ten years under the name of Circus Markus. Although Mack is strong man, knife-thrower, fire-eater and ringmaster as well as Whacko, the clown, he admits with a justifiable sense of pride that he can play nothing straight. His natural comicality enlivens his more serious acts—as does his skill in using audience participation. As Gunga Din, the strong man, glamorous in gold lamé, he takes ten men from the audience and seats them on a plank between two drums. He then attempts to lift the plank on the soles of his feet. Too heavy at one end? He takes a shoe from a man at one end of the plank and gives it to a man at the other for 'balance'. The audience grins at the absurdity of the idea, while Mack makes his second attempt. With an apparent ease which belies the back strain from which he suffers, he lifts what can be the equivalent of two and a half hundredweight (280 pounds).

As for his clowning act itself, Mack has no need to copy the 'Superman' or 'Incredible Hulk' parodies which have become common in some circus routines. His act depends almost entirely on the reactions of children he invites into the ring to try out a few acrobatic tricks with him. Any reluctant participant may find he is persuaded by a clownish whack on the head with a rolled-up newspaper from a grotesque, tattered figure in a long blond wig, outsize shoes and a bulbous nose. If audience response to him is anything to go by, Mack's own definition of a clown is not far off the mark; he believes a true clown has a personality that reaches out to people and makes them break into smiles even with the simplest piece of clown 'business'.

In the past, Circus Markus has employed outside artists—in one instance, an unemployed teacher who could hop up steps on one hand; but it has thrived best as a one-family show. Mack is helped by his devoted wife Shirley, an ex-chorus girl who worked with him when he left the big-time circus, into which he was born, for the holiday resort circuit. In addition to running up their first circus tent on her sewing machine and making all the costumes, Shirley is a stoical fall-girl to the clown and strong man. Two of their four young children

Soviet Russian clown Mickhail Rumyantsev in May 1976; as Karandash he developed the Russian school of 'realistic' clowning (*Novosti Press Agency*)

make very professional contributions to the show. Eleven-year-old Linda poses and somersaults across a tight-rope and performs aerial feats on a rope before being carried off on one hand by her father. Brian, now sixteen, juggles with Indian clubs or tennis balls, twirls a lasso with his teeth and balances a mountain of plastic tumblers. The two younger children, Julia and Amanda, have yet to make their debut. No circus would be complete without its animals, and Circus Markus boasts a bucking mule called Buckshot for the Peter Jenkins' bareback riding act and several Shetland ponies. There are two llamas, which are still in training, in addition to two goats, kept more for good luck than as performing animals.

But good luck is not what keeps Mack going; it is effort. He is an immensely hard-working man—his own driver, mechanic, carpenter, electrician, vet, sign-painter, booking-agent and tent boy, as well as the star performer. Despite hardships Mack and his family are too much in love with circus life ever to give up. 'You can't retire in this business. The minute you do, you die. You run a circus because you love it, because you're daft.'

If Mack seems his own man in business, he is certainly just as forceful in fending off the occasional do-gooder who arrives to inquire after the children's lack of conventional schooling. As far as he is concerned, people go to school to learn how to make their own living. But is not his entire family doing just that already? Referring to his own lack of formal education he says, 'If I'd had a good education, I'd be on the dole now'.

With today's higher expectations, it is more usual for clowns to send their children away to school or at least to see that they eventually have a choice between remaining in circus life or working in the outside world. Charlie Cairoli Junior, for instance, is a trained engineer as well as a fine clown. The auguste Tommy Fossett presents his two young sons, John and Tommy Junior, in the ring only during their school holidays. They take part in the straight Continental-style musical spots Tommy has introduced into his 'Professor Grimble' entrée.

Musical talent was once thought to be the hallmark of Continental clowns, whereas British clowns were more renowned for their acrobatic and slapstick comedy. Today, however, an increasing number of British clowns play several instruments well and use them as comically as did the memorable Grock. The veteran clown Alec Halls, who was made a Member of the Order of the British Empire for entertaining the forces in the Far and Middle East during World War II, plays eleven instruments. He is best known for his solo drum entrée, in which he scores a success by involving the audience in an 'Oh, no you can't!' 'Oh, yes I can'! routine as he repeatedly throws a drumstick into the air and attempts to catch it on its way down.

Don Sanders is the son of parents who planned a concert hall career for him, only to see him apply his musical talent to a clown routine involving bagpipes and piano, which became popular in theatres and circuses all over the globe. The father and son auguste team, Noe-Noe and Gary, are billed as musical clowns. Teddy Green claims to 'half-play' nine instruments and spends his spare time teaching himself the musical saw, that old stand-by of the music-hall comics.

An important difference between British and Continental clowns is the degree of personal prestige they enjoy. Continental clowns are not expected to concentrate on anything but the work they do in the ring. There is great respect for their artistry and many of them are very highly paid. Among the most popular

opposite above: Jacko the clown charms snakes (*Douglas Dickins*)
opposite below: Clown Cavalcade performer Brian Dewhirst plays to an audience in a London park, in the summer of 1977 (*Nick Birch*)

are Los Morenos, who—typically of most clown acts on the Continent—base their comedy on the interaction of the white clown and his two augustes. Juanito, father of the family was born in Spain in 1915 but is of Venezuelan nationality. Their act is a combination of music, slapstick and satire, which includes an hilarious parody of a fan dance. Other noted acts are the French Les Francescos and Les Chabri and the Italian Rastellis. The Rastellis were seen world-wide on television when they entertained Pope John Paul II in the Vatican on his return from a tour in South America in 1979.

The pope is not the only public figure to find pleasure in clowns. Prince Rainier of Monaco, who is a circus addict, invited the old clown Zozo to perform in his palace after the launch of the International Circus Festival in the principality in December 1974. Top-flight artists from all over the world have gathered here at subsequent winter festivals held under the prince's patronage. In 1979 the American and Canadian public were treated to the first touring show of the 'Festival International Cirque du Monte Carlo Spectacular'. The touring festival was launched by Irvin and Kenneth Feld, directors of Ringling Brothers and Barnum & Bailey. Following European tradition, the show was performed in a single ring, unlike the mammoth three-ring shows to which Americans are accustomed.

The sheer size of most American circuses has been blamed as the major factor preventing clowns from achieving public recognition. As in Europe, the star

214

system for clowns is extinct. With the death of Emmett Kelly in the spring of 1979, no clown in America today, with the possible exception of Lou Jacobs, would be instantly recognized. The clown hides in an anonymity which is part of the nature of American circus as it has evolved during the last fifty years.

Cut-throat competition among nineteenth-century proprietors had led to bigger and bigger circuses, some of them surrounded by hippodrome tracks. As far back as 1919, the newly-amalgamated Ringling-Barnum circus could seat 10,000 people in its enormous tent. Ninety railway carriages were needed to move the circus and 1,500 people to run it and perform in it. The enterprise well earned its title (borrowed from Barnum), 'The Greatest Show on Earth'.

This is not to say, however, that size is the hallmark of all American circuses. According to Bert Sikorsky of Clowns of America, Inc., there are about sixty circuses of all sizes in the country. Some of them employ only one clown, a white face; others use several: one tramp clown, one white face and the rest knockabout augustes. However, the majority of America's circus clowns are asked to put over their comedy in enormous areas, such as the colossal arena in Cleveland, Ohio, which holds more than 20,000 spectators.

The demise of the Big Top, as the Ringling tent was called, saddened many circus lovers, but it was inevitable. During the 1950s the circus was being hit by competition from big indoor pop concerts. At the same time suburbs were sprawling in all directions, and finding a suitable circus ground near a town centre was becoming more and more difficult. So 'The Greatest Show on Earth' abandoned the uneconomic canvas—preventing it, says its director Irvin Feld, 'from going the way of the Wild West show and the buffalo nickel'—and went indoors.

In the vast arenas now used only the acrobatic and pantomime clowns thrive; the talking and musical entrées which are appreciated more in the intimate atmosphere of smaller circuses or theatres are generally abandoned. Even with the use of microphones, clowns are very dependent on the visual joke; more subtle clowning would be lost in the topmost reaches of the audience.

The visual gags are usually identified with individual clowns. Lou Jacobs, for instance, uses a motorized bath and shower in his walkaround (the equivalent of the British run-in) and manages to scrub his back while 'driving to work'. Jacobs, a veteran auguste who joined Ringling Brothers and Barnum & Bailey in 1924, after leaving his native Germany, is easily recognized, even from a distance, thanks to his little dog Knucklehead, which he leads round the ring on an incongruously thick cable instead of the usual leash.

The longer sketches in the three-ring circus are known as production gags, and the clowns who devise and perform them are known as production clowns. Many command high prestige among their colleagues, as well as high salaries.

Lou Jacobs is one of the most experienced production clowns, and it is said that he has created more mechanical contraptions for his act than any other circus clown. His midget car is famous. Behind the scenes he will cram his six-foot-one-inch frame and enormous clown shoes into the car; then he will speed round the ring accompanied by numerous backfirings and midget policemen and finally emerge from the tiny vehicle to roars of laughter and disbelief. Jacobs' early career as a contortionist is obviously a great help to him, for the car is a mere yard long and a foot-and-a-half high.

A three-ring circus makes enormous demands on a clown. Not only does he perform his own entrée; he also takes part in several walkarounds and in the lavish parade, each of which requires quick costume changes. Enormous energy is needed to keep up a high standard of performance for fourteen shows a week, fifty weeks a year. The tough demands of circus life, as well as the growing competition from pop music and television, were no doubt responsible for the decline in the numbers entering the clown's profession during the 1950s and 60s. The possibility that the art of clowning might die out with the clowns themselves was averted largely through an innovation established by the 'Greatest Show' itself.

In 1968 director Irvin Feld founded the Clown College at the circus's winter quarters in Florida. The response was large; after the first course, the clown population of the circus rose from ten to a respectable sixty, with an average age of twenty-three. But however inventive these newcomers to the red nose and baggy pants may be, they have still to work within the limitations imposed by the three-ring structure and the show's philosophy of providing 'clean, wholesome, all-American entertainment'. One of the school's graduates is the clown, academic and writer, John H. Towsen. His thoughts about the future of clowning in the three-ring circus have a pessimistic flavour: '. . . it seems unlikely that the American [three-ring] circus clowns' approach to comedy will be significantly altered at any time in the near future.'

More subtle American clowning is represented by the Chaplinesque tramp clown, Joe Jackson Junior, who re-creates the act of his father. Joe Jackson Senior died in the 1940s. His best known sketch features a magnificent bicycle which the tramp comes upon and with alacrity decides to steal. When he tries to take the bike, it has other ideas and by degrees falls apart in his hands. Doggedly, the tramp sets about the task of putting the bike together, signalling as he does to his various emotions of frustration, sadness, anger and optimism. To his alarm, his ragged garments get caught in the machine's parts. Jackson, who was a brilliant mime, performed this act to packed houses in vaudeville and the earlier American one-ring circus, but it did not go down as successfully in the bigger arenas, where many of the finer points of his routine were lost.

With the death of vaudeville and the merging of many smaller circuses, opportunities for good clowns in America have become fewer, and attitudes towards them are not unlike the rather dismissive feeling in Britain. It may have a little to do with the disreputable, darker atmosphere of the old travelling circuses, whose owners were not above burning a bridge across a river or stream in order to force a rival to make a longer journey.

In his book on American circus clowns, *The World of Clowns*, George Bishop tells a story which illustrates the rather racy character of the old circuses before they came under the control of big business. The story is related by a veteran clown called Harry Ross who recalls working for a show that consisted of a horse act, one elephant, a camel and the clown. Business had become so bad that it looked very much as if the show would have to close. The night the owner announced the sad news to his circus, the camel died. This really seemed the catastrophe to top everything. But an advance agent for the circus had an idea. He visited the newspaper office of the town the circus was scheduled to visit next and explained to the editor that an event unheard-of in the annals of the circus had occurred. Although the circus performers were severely shaken, he said, the show would go on as promised. When pressed for details, the publicity man explained: 'It seems that the elephant and the camel have gotten into a fight and the elephant has killed the dromedary in a fit of rage'. He promised the

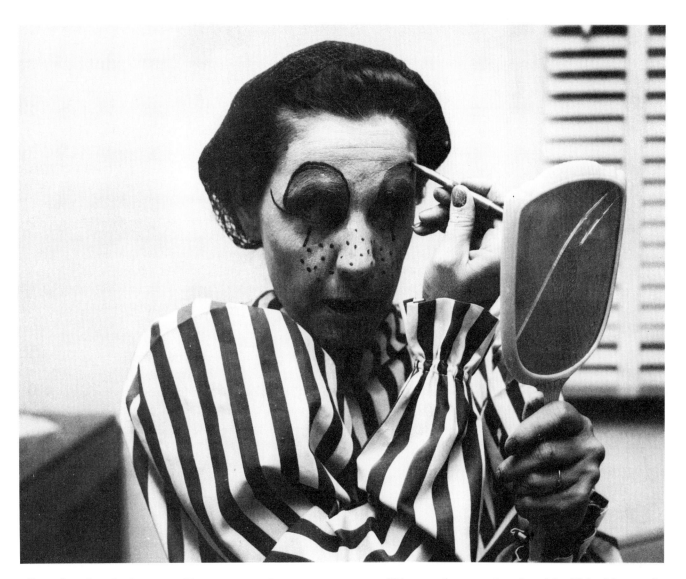

American Mrs Vicky Moore, who clowns under the name 'Todi', experiments with make-up (*John Topham Picture Library*)

editor that the elephant would present no danger to spectators if it were kept under canvas. However, it was too risky to parade the animal outside in the usual manner. Needless to say, seats for the circus were sold out the night the tale appeared in the newspaper, and the tent was full for the rest of the season. Everybody wanted to see the elephant who had killed the camel.

If a certain amount of ballyhoo has become associated with clowning in the mind of the American public, this was partly offset a few years ago when clowns were accorded some recognition from a somewhat unlikely source. In 1971, the then President Richard Nixon proclaimed National Clown Week, which has thereafter been held every year at the beginning of August. In the proclamation Nixon said, 'I urge the people of the United States to recognize the contributions made by the clowns in their entertainment at children's hospitals, charitable institutions, institutions for the mentally retarded, and generally helping to lift the spirits and boost the morale of our people'.

The slightly disparaging attitude towards circus and clowns in America and Europe is not found in the USSR. There, the circus arts are liberally subsidized by the government. One of the first things exported by the USSR when cultural exchanges with the West began was the Moscow State Circus. The writer

217

Faubion Bowers tells us that the nationalized circus is so highly esteemed in Moscow that it is accorded the lofty title, 'The Moscow Order of Lenin State Circus'. The school for clowns in Moscow has an academically serious atmosphere; and Russian circuses do not include the freaks, oddities and midgets which are still a part of circus elsewhere. Each member of the circus is respected for the skill which he or she contributes to what is, in effect, wholesome entertainment. Many of the great circus performers in Russia have been decorated, and nearly every city has a permanent circus building.

The modern Russian clown rarely portrays a poor or pathetic character. He is an anecdotist and comedian who is also fully trained in other circus arts. In the Soviet circus clowns often fulfil the same function as does the reprise clown in the West; that is, he appears after or during a serious turn and performs a comic parody of it. If the lion-tamer has put his wild beasts through their paces, the clown will appear to discipline a goose or a dog. The patter of the Russian clown often has a satirical bite, but such satire will often favour the Soviet Government's line. For example, during the Khrushchev era Oleg Popov devised a satirical sketch about avant-garde painters, then an officially approved target.

The Russian idea of realistic clowning was first developed by Karandash. Both he and Popov have been decorated by the government and enjoy as much fame as any star ballerina of the Bolshoi. Karandash has been featured in films and children's books and even represented in porcelain figurines. But while clowns of Soviet Russia enjoy great respect, they often seem to foreigners to be a little too serious. The comment of one foreign visitor to Russia reveals the very human need for just a little daftness to lighten the burden of life: 'As much as I admire these great clowns, I often hoped for a little more silliness from them, and, beyond that, something that would touch my heart. For me the element of fun or "pure pleasure" seems to be missing from Russian entertainment.'

This, then, is the clown in modern society. Generally speaking, clowns are finding their art less highly regarded than in the past and their traditional places of performance dwindling. Younger clowns are finding it harder to become apprenticed to the circus in the usual way and are taking to the streets, where a less disciplined, somewhat anarchic form of clowning is developing. Throughout history the clown has changed, yet remained essentially the same. Today he has modern technology to help him create more weird and wonderful props, but his humour finds its basis, as it has always done, in honest recognition of what it means to be human.

To conclude, here is a verse from a song by Randy Newman, the American songwriter:

> Find a clown
> And grind him down
> He may just be laughing at you
> And on principle
> An uncommitted man
> Can hardly be permitted
> To sit around and laugh
> At what the decent
> People try to do.
>
> (from 'Davy, the Fat Boy')

Bibliography

Armin, Robert, *Nest of Ninnies*, 1608

Barber, Cesar, *Shakespearian Festive Comedy*, Princeton University Press, 1959

Barrault, Jean-Louis, *Theatre of Jean-Louis Barrault*, Barrie and Rockcliff, London, 1961

Beare, W., *The Roman Stage*, Methuen & Co., London, 1950

Beaumont, C. W., *History of Harlequin*, London, 1926

Bishop, George, *The World of Clowns*, Brooke House Publishers, Los Angeles, 1976

Boorde, Andrew, *Scoggin's Jests*, W. Thackeray & J. Deacon, 1626

Bowers, Faubion, *Entertainment in Russia*, Thomas Nelson & Sons, New York, 1959

Broadbent, R. J., *A History of Pantomime*, Simkin, Marshall, London, 1901

Chancellor, F. Beresford, *Pleasure Haunts of London During Four Centuries*, Constable & Co., London, 1926

Chaplin, Charles, *My Autobiography*, Bodley Head, 1964

Croft-Cooke, Rupert and Meadmore, W. S., *Sawdust Ring*, Odhams, London, 1951

Croft-Cooke, Rupert (editor), *The Circus Book*, Sampson, Low, London, 1948

Dibdin, Charles, *The Professional Life of Charles Dibdin*, published by the author, 1803

— —, *Memoirs of Charles Dibdin the Younger*, edited by George Speaight, Society for Theatre Research, 1956

Disher, M. Willson, *Clowns and Pantomimes*, Constable & Co., London, 1925

— —, *Fairs, Circuses and Music-halls*, Collins, London, 1942

Doran, John, *History of Court Fools*, R. Bentley, London, 1858

Douce, Francis, *Illustrations of Shakespeare and Ancient Manners*, Longmans, London, 1807

Duchartre, Pierre Louis, *The Italian Comedy*, Dover Publications, New York, 1966

Findlater, Richard, *King of Clowns*, MacGibbon & Kee, 1955, new edition 1979

Fratellini, Albert, *Nous, les Fratellinis*, Bernard Grasset, Paris, 1955

Frost, Thomas, *Circus Life and Circus Celebrities*, Tinsley Bros., London, 1875

Goldsmith, R. H., *Wise Fools in Shakespeare*, Liverpool University Press, 1958

Grimaldi, Joseph, *Memoirs of Joseph Grimaldi*, edited by 'Boz', Richard Bentley, New Burlington Street, London, 1838 and 1846 editions

Grock, *Grock, King of Clowns*, Methuen, London, 1957

— —, *Life's a Lark*, Heinemann, London, 1931

Jusserand, A. A. J., *English Wayfaring Life in the Middle Ages*, T. Fisher Unwin, 1889 (original French edition, 1846)

Keaton, Buster, *My Wonderful World of Slapstick*, George Allen & Unwin, London, 1967

Kelly, Emmett, with Kelley, F. B., *Clown*, Prentice-Hall, New York, 1954

Knight, Dame Laura, *Oil, Paint and Greasepaint*, Nicolson & Watson, London, 1936

Kober, August Heinrich, *Star Turns*, Noel Douglas, London, 1928

Lahue, K. C., *World of Laughter*, University of Oklahoma Press, 1966

Lea, K. M., *Italian Popular Comedy*, Clarendon Press, Oxford, 1934

Lloyd, Harold C., *An American Comedy*, Longmans & Co., New York, 1928

— —, *Harold Lloyd's World of Comedy*, 1966

Luke, Sir Harry, *An Eastern Chequerboard*, Lovat Dickson, London, 1934

Mahood, M., *Shakespeare's Word Play*, Methuen & Co., London, 1957

Marceau, Marcel, *A la rencontre de la mime et des mimes Decroux, Barrault, Marceau*, published 1958

— —, *Marcel Marceau, ou L'aventure du silence*, published 1974

Mast, Gerald, *The Comic Mind*, published 1973

May, Earl Chapin, *The Circus From Rome to Ringling*, Duffield and Green, New York, 1932

Mayhew, Henry, *Selections from London Labour and the London Poor of 1851*, Pilot Press, London, 1949

Mills, Cyril W., *Bertram Mills Circus: its story*, Hutchinson, London, 1967

Morley, Henry, *Memoirs of St Bartholomew Fair*, Chapman & Hall, London, 1859

Nicoll, A., *Masks, Mimes and Miracles*, Harrap, London, 1931

— —, *The World of Harlequin*, Cambridge University Press, 1963

Palmer, J., *Comic Characters of Shakespeare*, MacMillan & Co., London, 1945

Pinks, William J., *History of Clerkenwell*, C. Herbert, London, 1881

Poliakoff, Nicolai (Coco the Clown), *Behind My Greasepaint*, Hutchinson, London, 1950

——, *Coco the Clown: By Himself*, Dent, London, 1940

Pope, Walter J. Macqueen, *Ghosts and Greasepaint*, Robert Hale, London, 1951

Popov, Oleg, *Russian Clown*, English translation, 1970

Remy, Tristan, *Entrées clownesques*, Paris, 1962

Reynolds, Butch, *Broken-hearted Clown*, Arco Publications, London, 1954

Rivels, Charlie, *Poor Clown*

Sand, Maurice, *The History of the Harlequinade*, Secker, London, 1915

Sanders, Ruth Manning, *The English Circus*, Werner Laurie, London, 1952

Sanger, Lord George, *Seventy Years a Showman*, Dent, 1938, original edition published by C. Arthur Pearson, 1908

Sennett, Mack, *King of Comedy*, Peter Davies, London, 1955

Sitwell, Osbert, *The Four Continents*, Macmillan, London, 1954

Smith, Lady Eleanor Furneaux, *Life's a Circus*, Longmans, London, 1939

Speaight, George, *The History of the English Puppet Theatre*, Harrap, 1955

Tarlton, Richard, *Tarlton's Jests*, London Shakespeare Society edition, 1884

Thompson, C. J. S., *Quacks of Old London*, Brentano's, London, 1928

Thoms, W. J., *Anecdotes and Traditions*, Camden Society, London, 1839

Towsen, John H., *Clowns*, Hawthorn Books Inc., 1976

Vitry, Jacques de, *Histoire des Croisades*, 1218

Wallett, W. F., *The Public Life of William Wallett, The Queen's Jester*, Bemrose & Sons, London

Weaver, John, *History of Mimes and Pantomimes*, London, 1728

Weiss, John, *Wit and Humour of Shakespeare*, Boston, Cambridge, 1876

Welsford, Enid, *The Fool*, Faber and Faber, London, 1935

Wheatley, Henry B., *London Past and Present*, Murray, London, 1891

Whimsical Walker, *From Sawdust to Windsor Castle*, Stanley Paul, London, 1922

Index